Godly Women, Godly Calls

The Stories of Six Women Used Powerfully by God

Deena S. Jones

AmErica House
Baltimore

© 2001 by Deena S. Jones.
All rights reserved. No part of this book may be reproduced in any form without written permission from the publishers, except by a reviewer who may quote brief passages in a review to be printed in a newspaper or magazine.

First printing

Unless otherwise indicated, all scripture references are from the New American Standard Bible, Copyright The Lockman Foundation 1960, 1962, 1963, 1968, 1971, 1972, 1973, 1975, 1977, 1995. Used by permission.

ISBN: 1-58851-442-0
PUBLISHED BY AMERICA HOUSE BOOK PUBLISHERS
www.publishamerica.com
Baltimore

Printed in the United States of America

I dedicate this book
to my beloved husband Chris,
whose support and encouragement
have been vital to my success.

Table of Contents

Introduction 7

Joan of Arc 11

Sojourner Truth 27

Aimee Semple McPherson 47

Uldine Utley 65

Corrie ten Boom 69

Kathryn Kuhlman 85

End Notes 97

Works Cited 107

Introduction

The Lord gives the command; The women who proclaim the good tidings are a great host.
  – Psalm 68: 11 NASB

As a woman called into ministry, I have found myself caught up in the same struggle that all women in ministry face – a challenge to our legitimacy. As an evangelical, the need to understand the pertinent biblical passages, those that seem to exclude women from serving as pastors or in leadership roles, becomes more acute. I once asked one of my more liberal sisters how she deals with the challenges to her right to serve, and she replied, "When people ask me about that I just say, 'Oh, that's just Paul and I don't like him anyway.'" Apparently, she has no trouble dismissing out of hand those biblical passages she finds troubling, but that doesn't work for me. I consider the entire Bible to be the inspired Word of God.

So, the problem comes down to how to deal with these passages that seem to contradict other parts of the Bible. I'm sure I've seen every argument on the subject, and yet I am still not entirely convinced that anyone has fully found the answer.

Some of the arguments in favor of women in ministry, I must admit, look suspiciously like exegetical gymnastics. Yet, to accept the passages at face value in our current English translations, as some insist that we must, creates more problems. How can we understand *1 Tim. 2: 12*, for example, in relation to *Galatians 3: 28*? How is it that women are placed under bondage to the law, while men have been set free in Christ?

I believe that God is a God who makes sense. I don't believe

He gifts certain people for service and then forbids them to use their gifts. Furthermore, I see the Apostle Paul as a man who wanted nothing more than to see people come to Christ. His whole life after his conversion was dedicated to spreading the gospel of Jesus Christ, and he would use whatever means necessary to get the message across. He said, "To the Jews I became as a Jew, that I might win Jews; to those who are under the Law, as under the Law, though not being myself under the Law, that I might win those who are under the Law; to those who are without law, as without law…that I might win those who are without law. To the weak I became weak, that I might win the weak; I have become all things to all men, that I may by all means save some" (*1 Cor. 9: 20-22*). It makes no sense to me that Paul would then silence some people and forbid them to spread the gospel of Jesus Christ. It strikes me as contrary to his whole purpose for being. For that reason, I honestly believe that Paul and his writings have been misunderstood for centuries.

Paul welcomed the help of women. He mentions Euodia and Syntyche who "labored with me in the gospel" (*Phil. 4: 3, NKJV*). The New American Standard Bible reads: "contended with me." His lists of greetings frequently include women who were an active part of his ministry.

Paul was strategic in his work. He would go to major centers of commerce to plant the seeds of the gospel, and he would always go to the Jews first, preaching in the synagogues until he was thrown out. In Philippi, there apparently was no synagogue, so *Acts 16: 13* says that Paul and his companions went instead outside the city to a place of prayer and they spoke to the women who were gathered there. Why waste their time preaching the gospel to women, if the women would be forbidden to spread the good news to the rest of the city? Lydia, a businesswoman, is the first convert and Paul establishes his base of operation in her home.

The purpose of this book is not to re-examine the controversial Bible passages and the exegetical discussions that have ensued. I leave that to those whose minds are better suited for it than mine. My purpose, rather, is to show how God was at work in the lives of a few women who responded to what they genuinely believed was God's call and who made a difference in the lives of the people they touched. Readers who don't believe God would ever place a woman in a position of authority over men, or send a woman to preach the gospel, may reach different conclusions than I have reached. However, I hope people will keep an open mind and examine the evidence.

The women I have chosen to write about come from a variety of backgrounds and lived in different times. None of them was perfect. They each had their struggles and moments of failure, but they also had something else in common: they were totally yielded to God. God was able to use them in a powerful way because they were willing to be used. They, like Paul, wanted nothing more than to be of service to God and to give their lives for the call that God had placed before them. Anyone, whether male or female, who wants to be used by God must be willing to surrender to His will.

Women in ministry are often looked upon with suspicion. Some consider them to be power hungry, and grasping an authority they were not meant to have, and so they are forced to defend their call. Kathryn Kuhlman offered this advice for women in ministry. She said, "Let women be sure – very sure – that they have a call from God before they ever decide to enter such a ministry. If you are not definitely called, don't do it."[1] That would be good advice for anyone. Why try to do something that God is not orchestrating? However, if God is calling you and equipping you for ministry, then go for it. Do what God tells you to do, and let the naysayers disapprove all they want. God is the One we have to answer to.

Joan of Arc

But God has chosen the foolish things of the world to shame the wise, and God has chosen the weak things of the world to shame the things which are strong.
– Corinthians 1: 27

"Blessed are the pure in heart, for they shall see God."
– Matthew 5: 8

If you were in need of someone to lead a military expedition against a mighty army, whom would you choose? What would you look for in a leader? Proven ability. Years of experience. Great physical stamina. Most likely, you would look for someone who had proven himself on the battlefield and who devised battle strategies with great cunning.

God tells us that His ways are not our ways. The Bible tells us He took a shepherd boy, the youngest of his father's sons, and made him king over all of Israel (*I Sam. 16: 1-13*). God took Gideon's army and reduced it to 300 men before He let them go into battle against a much larger force (*Judges 7*). God wanted everyone to know that He was the one who gave the victory.

One of the assessors at Joan of Arc's Trial of Condemnation stated that he did not believe that she was from God because God would not have chosen someone of such humble status to use as His instrument. Obviously, the Scriptures give us numerous examples of God doing precisely that.

Was Joan of Arc sent by God, or were the voices she heard demonic in origin, figments of her own imagination, or the results of schizophrenia? Everything we know about Joan comes to us from the court records of her trials. These include signed depositions of eyewitnesses, as well as testimony given under direct questioning.

Joan of Arc was born in a small French village called Domremy. The exact date of her birth is unknown, since such things were not recorded for peasants. However, 1412 seems to be the most likely year of her birth. Her father, Jacques d'Arc, although a peasant, was a prominent citizen in Domremy.

Joan never learned to read and write. Her education consisted of those things considered necessary for young girls to learn, such as spinning and sewing, as well as saying her prayers. In addition to helping around the house, Joan also tended her father's animals. It was during such times, when she was supposed to be tending the flock, that she would hear a nearby church bell ring and she would leave the animals to go to church. People who knew her well in her childhood later testified to her piety.

Joan no doubt was aware of what was happening in her country. France and England had been at war for decades before she was born, and so she grew up in a nation that was under enemy occupation. They lived with the threat of soldiers passing through towns, raping and looting as they went.

It all started when Charles IV, King of France, died without a male heir in 1328. The king's younger sister Isabella had married Edward II of England, and had given birth to Edward III, King of England. French law prevented the throne from being passed to females or through their line. However, England had no such law and chose not to recognize the law in France. Therefore, Edward III laid claim to the throne of France through his mother. The French, on the other hand, crowned Philip VI, first cousin to Charles IV, and the Hundred Years War began.

At the time of Joan's childhood, Henry V of England and Charles VI of France were continuing the age-old fight. Henry was a skilled warrior, while Charles suffered from bouts of madness. The stability of Charles' kingdom was further disrupted by the unfaithfulness and treachery of his wife, Isabeau of Bavaria[2]. On May 21, 1420 the Treaty of Troyes was signed, which allowed Charles VI to remain on the throne of France, but at his death the throne would pass to Henry V and his heirs. Thus, Charles and Isabeau agreed to disinherit their own son, the Dauphin Charles, whose legitimacy was often questioned, in light of Isabeau's infidelity. Within a short time, Henry V and Charles VI were both dead. Henry's infant son Henry VI was declared to be king of both England and France. Such was the state of affairs when Joan came on the scene of history.

When Joan was around the age of thirteen, she began hearing voices in her mind. The voices were accompanied by visions of shapes and light. They were identified to her as the Archangel Michael, and two martyred saints, Saint Catherine and Saint Marguerite. The two saints were to be her constant companions for the rest of her short life.

The voices gave Joan an assignment. She was to raise the siege on the city of Orleans, and to have the Dauphin crowned at Rheims. Further prophecies were given that Paris was to be recaptured and that the Duke of Orleans would be released from captivity in England.[3] Furthermore, all of the English who survived the war would be driven off of French soil.

Joan responded with as much hesitation as Moses, or more so. She was only a child, and a female child at that. What did she know about military strategy? Why should anyone listen to her? Besides all that, the city of Orleans was not under siege, nor ever likely to be so.

Joan dragged her feet for three years, until her voices became more insistent and stressed upon her the urgency of her mission. However, a young lady in medieval France did not simply leave her home and run off to join the army. Joan's father had had a dream in which he saw her riding with the army and he declared that he would rather see her drowned. Consequently, getting away required a bit of deception. An opportunity arose when she was invited to visit relatives in a nearby town. She was able to persuade her relative Durand Laxart of the earnestness of her mission, and he agreed to take her to Vaucouleurs to see Sir Robert de Baudricourt, a captain in the Dauphin's army.

Having previously been warned that Baudricourt would not listen to her until she had visited him three times, Joan was really not surprised when he sent her away, strongly urging Laxart to return her to her father and administer a sound thrashing to keep her from behaving so again. This first visit was in May of 1428,[4] when Joan was approximately 16 years old. She did return home, but she prophesied that before the next Lent was over, she must be with the Dauphin. In October of 1428, the English had indeed laid siege to Orleans.

Another opportunity to go to Vaucouleurs presented itself when Laxart's wife became pregnant and requested Joan's presence for the birth, which would be during the following Lent. Joan was able to speak with Baudricourt a second time, and was rebuffed again. However, superstition ran high in Medieval Europe. Rumors had spread that a young maiden was petitioning to speak with the Dauphin, saying she was from God and that she had been sent to liberate France. The very rumors were enough to awaken hope in the hearts of the loyal French.

However, Baudricourt wanted to be sure that she was indeed from God and not from the devil. He and a priest went to see her, to exorcise any demons that may have possessed her. They left again, finding no evidence that she was possessed.

Finally, on Feb. 12, 1429, she chided Baudricourt for his delay in sending her to the Dauphin, saying that that very day France had suffered a serious setback. It was later learned that on that Feb. 12, which has been referred to as "The Day of the Herrings,"[5] the French forces had suffered a terrible defeat. Shortly after that, Joan was summoned to Chinon to appear before the Dauphin.

The journey was long and passed through dangerous territory. It was later reported that there were men-at-arms lying in wait to capture Joan on her journey, but they were mysteriously unable to strike when the time came, so she passed on unmolested.[6] Similarly, the men traveling with her testified that although Joan was attractive and they saw more of her skin than they should have, they had no carnal desire for her. Many people considered her safe arrival in Chinon as a miracle.

The rumors about Joan, who was now being referred to as "the Maid," doubtless had reached the Dauphin's ears. He had heard she was a prophet, so he began by putting her to a small test. He hid himself among his courtiers to see if she would know him. She, upon entering the room, went immediately to Charles, although she had never seen him before. She told him of her mission, and he drew her aside for private conversation. There she told him something that made his face light up with joy,[7] and which caused him to believe she was indeed sent from God. Years later the Dauphin confided that one day, in a sorrowful mood because of all his troubles, he prayed a silent prayer, asking God to protect him and to show him whether or not he was the legitimate king. On Joan's first visit, she repeated the prayer to him.[8]

The Dauphin was not content to judge Joan himself, so he had her examined by many learned theologians at Poitiers. Unfortunately, if records were kept of the inquiry, they have never been found. One of the men testified at Joan's trial of rehabilitation, giving some of the questions that were asked of her. After she had been thoroughly examined, she was declared to be truly acting by the will of God and that to obstruct her in any way would be an "offense to the Holy Spirit."[9]

In addition to this theological examination, Joan was also examined in an entirely different manner. The king gave certain women the task of determining if Joan was indeed a virgin. They reported that she was physically intact. This was of major importance, because a woman acting on behalf of the devil would have lost her virginity long since.

When the Dauphin was completely satisfied that Joan's mission was pure, he consented to give her an army, outfitting her with armor and a horse. Her voices had told her to use a sword that would be found buried behind the altar in a chapel dedicated to Saint Catherine. It was found exactly where they said it would be, with another blade that had belonged to Charles Martel, who had delivered France from the threat of the Infidel.[10] How Joan's sword came to be there remains a mystery.

In keeping with her stated mission, Joan was sent to Orleans to raise the siege. The Dauphin had provided her with a suit of armor and a horse and had commissioned her, an inexperienced girl of 17, a captain in his army. She had her own standard, a white banner depicting Christ holding a Fleur-de-lys. She also had a banner made for Jean Pasquerel, her confessor, for the purpose of rallying the priests. On the march to Orleans, she put the priests in front of the army, where they went singing hymns, much as Jehoshaphat had done in *2 Chron. 20: 21-22*.

The raising of the siege at Orleans was miraculous from start to finish. As Joan arrived at Orleans, bringing provisions with her, the English, who were not the least bit shy about using their weapons, never fired a shot. In addition, an unfavorable wind changed when she arrived, making the army's entry possible.

Whereas, the very presence of the Maid brought hope to the French army and the people of Orleans, the English captains knew they must convince their men that she was a witch and not from God at all, or else they would completely lose heart for the battle. They insisted she was a whore. One fellow called her such a name to her face. She tearfully replied that he was offending God and would soon be dead. The man died a few days later, when he fell from a burning bridge. Similarly, another man made a bawdy joke, threatening to take Joan's virginity. She said, "Do you offend God who are so soon to die?" Within an hour, the man drowned.[11]

While at Orleans, Joan was awakened very early one morning by her voices that told her that the battle had begun. She jumped up, shouting at her page to hurry up, and then rode off to join the battle. Joan had always insisted that her men confess their sins to a priest before they go into battle. Therefore, she wept bitterly when she saw Englishmen being slain, as she did not know if they had been given the same opportunity.

Joan had predicted that she would be wounded at Orleans. She told Jean Pasquerel that blood would flow out of her body above her breast.[12] As predicted, she was struck by an arrow above her breast and was taken off the battlefield. Immediately the English began to gain the advantage. Joan insisted that her wound be quickly bandaged and her armor returned to her, so she could return to the battle. The sight of her returning completely discomfited the English. They had always been told that a witch loses her powers when she sees her own blood, and here she was returning to the battlefield, little worse for wear. Near the end of the battle, the English supposedly had a vision of two patron saints of Orleans, accompanied by Saint Michael, leading the French army.[13]

The siege of Orleans, which had lasted for several months, came to an end in just a few days after Joan's arrival. The people of Orleans credited her with the victory. She knew that the victory belonged to God.

In spite of the speedy victory at Orleans, Joan had a difficult time convincing the Dauphin to act on the second part of her mission, his crowning at Rheims. For some reason, he was reluctant to go through with it, but he eventually gave in. They had to fight their way to Rheims, capturing various towns as they went. One was the city of Troyes. Of that battle the Bastard of Orleans, who had followed Joan after the victory at Orleans, testified thus:

> Then the Maid arrived and entered the council chamber, saying more or less these words: 'Noble Dauphin, command your people to come and besiege the city of Troyes, and drag out your debates no longer. For in God's name, within three days I will lead you into the city of Troyes, by love, force, or courage, and that false Burgundy will be quite thunderstruck.' Then the Maid immediately went over with the King's army, and pitched her camp alongside the moat. The positions that she took up were so admirable that even the two or three most famous and experienced captains would not have made as good a plan of battle. Indeed, the work that she did that night was so effective that the next day the bishop and citizens of the city offered their allegiance to the King, in fear and trembling. And it was learnt later that from the moment when she had given the King her advice not to go away from the city, the inhabitants had lost heart.[14]

Charles VII was crowned in Rheims on July 16, 1429. Joan's father was in attendance, an indication that he had forgiven her for her disobedience.

Some have wondered what might have happened if Joan had declared her mission accomplished and returned home at this time, rather than continuing to fight for the liberation of France. It is thought that she had now tasted the glory of war and believed herself indispensable to the army of France. Joan had expressed a wish to retire from public life after the coronation, but she said she went to Paris at the request of her comrades in arms. She said her actions were "neither against nor at the command of my voices."[15]

However, after Rheims, victories did not come as easily as they did before. Joan and her soldiers complained of much idleness as they sat around waiting for the King to act. Rather than marching on Paris immediately, while they had the momentum behind them, the King chose to squander the opportunity and wait. Unknown to Joan, he had entered into a treaty with his enemy, the Duke of Burgundy, on the understanding that Paris would be handed over to him without a fight. Burgundy and his cohort, the English Duke of Bedford, who was acting as regent for the child Henry VI, were simply buying time to reinforce their position. They had no intention of handing Paris to Charles.[16] Charles was also receiving traitorous advice from one of his courtiers, his favorite, La Tremoille.

One victory came at the town of Saint-Pierre-les-Moutiers. The French were being pressed hard and forced to retreat. Jean d'Aulon, testifying, said that he went to Joan to encourage her to retreat with the rest, since only four or five men remained with her. She refused to leave, saying she still had 50,000 men with her. She ordered wood to be brought and a bridge built, which was speedily done, and the town fell with very little resistance.[17]

The crowning of the King at Rheims caused several towns to return their loyalty to their rightful king. One such town was Beauvais. Everyone who would not swear allegiance to Charles VII was invited to leave. Bishop Pierre Cauchon, who was governor of Beauvais, was forced to leave. He would later become the leading judge at Joan's trial of condemnation.

The King's army finally went into battle against Paris in

September of 1429. Joan's voices had warned her not to go into battle on the 8th of September, but for once, she ignored them. She was wounded in the battle. Her troops were then demoralized, while her enemies were encouraged at the sight of her fall. Although Joan insisted they stay and fight under cover of darkness, La Tremoille called a retreat and the battle was abandoned.

Rumor had it that the city would have surrendered had they held out through the night, but the King's advisors won over Joan's arguments. Feeling very much defeated, she asked to be relieved of her duties to return to a life of obscurity, but the King would not give her leave.

Joan's voices warned her that she would be captured, and on May 23, 1430, she was taken during a battle outside Compiegne. Her enemies were overjoyed at this turn of events. She was held as the prisoner of John of Luxembourg. The English petitioned over and over again for Joan to be turned over to them, but John had promised his aged aunt that he would not do that. However, the old lady died in November of that year, and John of Luxembourg wasted no time in selling Joan into the hands of the English.

The English were still very eager to prove that Joan was a witch or a heretic, in order to relieve their soldiers' fears. Consequently, they insisted that she be tried as a prisoner of the Church and not as a political prisoner. However, as a prisoner of the Church, she should have been held in a convent or church prison, to be guarded by women, but she was not. She was held in a castle and guarded by male ruffians, who never ceased to molest her. During her incarceration, many men attempted to rape her. The fact that they failed can only be considered another miracle of God.

Joan was again examined by women, to establish her virginity, although this time the Duke of Bedford was peeking through a hole. His wife was one of the examining women. On finding that Joan was intact, she gave orders that the guards not take her virginity, though they still felt free to molest her. For this reason, Joan refused to wear women's clothing and continued to wear men's garb, as it offered her more protection from these unwanted advances.

In preparation for her trial, Pierre Cauchon, who was leading the trial, sent men to Domremy to inquire of Joan's childhood. Everything they uncovered was favorable to Joan, so Cauchon suppressed the reports, including the report of the women on Joan's virginity and a report from the findings at Poitiers.

The trial began in January of 1431 and lasted for several months, during which time Joan was often questioned for many hours at a time. Sometimes the assessors would run their questions together or talk at once, and she had to request them to speak one person at a time. In spite of her lack of education and the complexity of the questions, she managed to answer remarkably well. Sometimes she would request time to consult with her voices before answering, saying she would be glad to give an answer the next day.

Like our Lord, Joan had a way of turning the tables on those who meant to trap her, trapping them instead. Cauchon, attempting to prove her a witch or a heretic, commanded her to recite Pater Noster and Ave Maria. She replied that she would willingly do so, provided he first heard her confession. This put Cauchon, a priest, in an awkward position. If he heard her confession, he could not then pronounce her guilty. However, if he refused, he was failing to fulfill his priestly office.[18] This became a sticking point throughout the trial.

The proceedings of the trial were irregular from start to finish. Guillaume Manchon, the principle scribe at the trial, reported that Cauchon frequently instructed him to change Joan's answers and falsify the report, which Manchon refused to do. Two other scribes were hidden behind a curtain and kept a report that was very different from Manchon's, but on further examination, it was discovered that Manchon's version was correct.[19]

Another man, Jean de la Fontaine, stood in for Cauchon as Joan's questioner and suggested that she submit herself to the Pope, which she agreed to do. When Cauchon heard that she had appealed to the Pope he became very angry and threatened violence. La Fontaine fled the city and did not return.

One lawyer, Jean Lohier, told the court reporter that the entire proceeding was invalid for several reasons. He concluded by saying, "In matters touching her apparitions, she says: 'I know for certain' – whereas, if she had merely said, 'it seems to me' – in my opinion not a single man in all that lot would have the effrontery to find her guilty. If you ask me, they are animated by hatred and by nothing else – and that is why I am not going to remain. I do not want to have anything further to do with it. They don't like what I say."[20] More than sixty assessors likewise refused to continue and did not attend the last sessions.

An archdeacon declared that the trial was invalid. He was no longer invited to attend. Another fellow tried to get out of the trial and was threatened with his life if he did not attend. He remarked that the spectre of death hung over anyone who did not do as the English wished, who, by the way, were paying all the expenses of the trial.[21]

Joan was accused on seventy articles, but her answers supported none of them. Cauchon decided to simplify things by reducing the charges to twelve and leaving out the questions and Joan's answers entirely.[22] This was what was shown to the assessors and the University of Paris, who rendered their opinion based on that alone.[23]

Joan was convicted of heresy, but was given the opportunity to repent and to return to the true faith. A major issue was the wearing of men's clothing. If she were to confess that the voices she heard were not from God and if she should resume wearing women's clothing, there would be hope for her eternal soul.

There is some disagreement as to whether Joan of Arc actually confessed. In order to wring a confession out of her, she was taken on May 24, 1431 to the cemetery of Saint-Ouen where a scaffold had been prepared for her burning. She was forced to listen to a lengthy, harsh sermon and then was offered a choice. If she confessed, she would be taken to a women's prison where she would live the rest of her days. If she did not, she would be burned on the spot.

A written confession had been prepared for her and read to her, which she eventually signed. However, that piece of paper disappeared and another, much lengthier paper was inserted in the trial records. Those who were present later testified that the document in the records was not the same as the document that Joan signed.[24] The signature on the second document was believed to be a forgery.

The testimony of the witnesses to Joan's signature are contradictory. Some say that she signed, but Haimond de Macy testified that the secretary Laurent Calot grabbed Joan's hand with the pen and made her sign.[25]

Later, Joan herself would admit that she had sinned a great sin in signing the document, though she said she did not fully understand what was in it. She said she acted out of fear of the fire and God was very displeased. However, she repented of her sin and was assured of God's pardon.

Contrary to what she had been promised, Joan was returned to her same prison cell with her same ruffian guards. She had been commanded to wear women's clothing and she had agreed, believing she would be guarded henceforth by women. When she was returned to her cell she realized that she had been tricked.

The following Sunday, Joan was back in her male clothes. One witness testified that the guards had taken her female clothing away and gave her only male clothing, which she was finally forced to put on because of "the necessity of the body." Joan gave as her reason for resuming the male clothing that she had been lied to and had been returned to her same prison with male guards and was still in chains. She had decided death was preferable to life in that prison. Whatever her reason, Cauchon was overjoyed because this was the evidence he needed to prove that she was a relapsed heretic. In addition to wearing the male clothing, Joan had also recanted her confession of a few days previous. Cauchon laughed as he said to the Englishmen, "Farewell. Be of good cheer. It is done."[26]

On Monday, Joan was immediately tried for relapse, with the finding on the following day that she was guilty. Early Wednesday morning, May 30, 1431, Joan's sentence of death was pronounced upon her. She was taken at once to the Old Market Place in Rouen and supposedly handed over to civil authorities. However, no civil sentence was ever pronounced upon her, as everyone seemed to be in a hurry to have her burned.

Although Joan had declared that she had been wrongly treated, that had she been turned over to an ecclesiastical prison, to be guarded by women, she would not have resumed the male garb, still she forgave the Englishmen for what they had done. She went to the stake with much lamentation and prayers, calling on the Trinity, the Holy Virgin, and all the saints to help her. Those who witnessed her death said they could hear her constant prayers and cries to God as she suffered. She died with the name "Jesus" on her lips.

Witnesses were very much affected by her death. Some of the English made a profession of faith after seeing her piety to the end. Another Englishman ran from the fire screaming that he had seen a dove fly from her mouth as she died. The executioner was terrified that he was forever damned for having burnt a saint. He avowed that no amount of oil, charcoal or sulfur could make her heart or entrails burn.[27]

A few years after Joan's death, Paris was recaptured by the French and on June 17, 1452 the Hundred Years War came to an end, with the rest of the English being totally driven out, as Joan had predicted.

Rouen, where Joan was tried and killed, was recaptured by the French in 1449. Charles VII was then able to recover all the documents of Joan's trial. He immediately set up an inquiry into the nature of the trial.

The current pope, Nicholas V, had no desire to stir up trouble between England and France, or to anger either of their kings, so he did very little with regards to the trial. His successor, Calixtus III was completely impartial and agreed to conduct an inquiry, as had been requested by Joan's mother and brothers.

Joan's Trial of Rehabilitation, during which many witnesses from her childhood and from her army were called to testify, found that the former trial was completely invalid and illegally conducted. Joan's appeal to the Pope should have been honored, as he should have been the one to judge whether or not the voices were from God. In the end, her execution was declared to have been murder[28] and Joan herself was declared to be clean of "any taint of infamy."[29] Five hundred years after her death, Joan was canonized on May 9, 1920.

Was Joan of Arc sent by God or was she an instrument of the devil? Everyone who knew her personally believed her to have been a very pious and godly young woman. The Dauphin Charles and the doctors of theology at Poitiers found no fault in her. Every prophecy she pronounced was fulfilled exactly as she said it would be. The men who fought at her side believed the victories they achieved were miracles of God and not wrought by human hands. Even many of the assessors at her trial of condemnation could not believe that she was evil and so they refused to continue to participate in the trial.

The only people who declared her to be acting on behalf of the devil were those men who had an ulterior motive. They were in the pay of her mortal enemies, and for all they might claim that hers was a trial of the Church, she was for all intents and purposes a political prisoner, a prisoner of war.

There is absolutely no evidence that Joan was possessed by a demon. If she was not from God, nor working for the devil, it follows that she was simply acting on her own behalf. Maybe the voices she heard were the result of mental illness. However, they told her to do things that she did not want to do. Also, they were remarkably accurate in their predictions. To believe that a simple country girl could accomplish militarily what she accomplished, with very little training and no experience is simply more than I can do. Faith, for me, is not blind but based on historical fact.

The facts in the case of Joan of Arc are clear enough. Only God could have coordinated the brilliant military achievements with which Joan is credited. She trusted completely in God and in God alone. When the men around her wouldn't believe her or listen to her advice, she would cry out to God and she would hear a voice say, "Go, child of God, go, go! Go and I will help you."[30]

Joan of Arc was obedient unto death. I would like to think that her final cry of "Jesus" came not as a plea, but as a welcome, as she saw Him face to face, much like Stephen, who said he could see Jesus "standing at the right hand of God" (*Acts 7: 56*).

Believing that Joan was from God requires a belief that God does in fact perform miracles and concern Himself with the goings-on of humans, since her accomplishments were military victories. Without God at her side, it is too hard to believe that she could have been able to do what she did. Her steadfast faith to her very last earthly breath proves to me that she was indeed a child of God.

Sojourner Truth

But we have this treasure in earthen vessels, that the surpassing greatness of the power may be of God and not from ourselves; we are afflicted in every way, but not crushed; perplexed, but not despairing; persecuted, but not forsaken; struck down, but not destroyed.
– 2 Corinthians 4: 7-9

"Blessed are those who hunger and thirst for righteousness, for they shall be satisfied."
– Matthew 5: 6

Sojourner Truth began life as a slave, but ended it as a national hero. She never sought fame, fortune, or glory for herself, but she traveled around the country, telling people about God's love and encouraging them to do what was right.

Sojourner, named Isabella at birth, was born somewhere around the year 1797, a slave of Colonel Hardenbergh of Ulster County, New York. Her mother was Elizabeth, also called Mau Mau, and her father was James, known as Baumfree, a Dutch word, meaning tree, because of his tall, straight stature. Mau Mau and Baumfree had many children, perhaps as many as thirteen, but all except Isabella and her younger brother Peter had been sold away. Mau Mau kept their memory alive by repeating stories of the lost children to Isabella and Peter.

The family lived in the cellar underneath the Hardenberghs' house, with the other slaves. The cellar was damp, with nothing but a few planks and straw to cover the dirt. Men and women were housed together in this disagreeable situation.

At the death of Colonel Hardenbergh, the slaves became the

property of his son Charles Hardenbergh. When he died unexpectedly, however, they were put on the auction block with all the rest of Col. Hardenbergh's "cattle."

Caring for aging slaves had always been a problem, and the Hardenbergh heirs knew that Baumfree's useful days were behind him. They knew they would not be able to sell him and none of them wanted to be responsible for his care, so they decided to give Mau Mau her freedom so that she could look after him. Isabella and Peter, however, went to the auction block.

At first, no one would bid on Isabella. Finally the auctioneer called for half a dozen sheep to be put with the girl, and he sold the lot for $100 to John Neely. John Neely had never owned a slave. He had been more interested in the sheep, but he thought the girl might be useful to his wife, so Isabella headed to her new home.

Isabella spoke only Dutch, the language of the Hardenberghs, but her new master and mistress only spoke English. Mrs. Neely had no patience at all with the girl. She took her lack of response to be insolence, and so Isabella was often beaten. Isabella struggled to be obedient, but she simply couldn't understand her mistress' instructions. One time, Mr. Neely beat her so hard he left scars that she would carry all of her life.

Isabella had learned from her mother that there is a God in heaven who watches over us and who sees all that we do. She had taught Isabella the Lord's Prayer, and told Isabella to pray whenever she was in trouble. Isabella prayed to God, asking Him to send her a new master. She also spoke to her earthly father, who, as a free man, came to visit her, asking him to try to get her a new master. Shortly thereafter, a gentleman by the name of Martin Schryver bought her for $105.

Schryver owned a tavern and a small farm. Isabella's workload was not heavy, and she was as contented as a person in bondage can be, but her time with the Schryvers proved to be short. John Dumont offered the equivalent of $300 for her, which was too much for the Schryvers to refuse. Once again, Isabella found herself with a new master. The year was 1810 and Mr. Dumont estimated her age to be between 12 and 14 years.

Mr. Dumont was well satisfied with his purchase, but Mrs. Dumont was less so. She continually found fault with Isabella's work. One of Isabella's tasks was to prepare potatoes for the family's breakfast. When the potatoes appeared gray and dirty, she was accused of not cleaning the potatoes properly. The next day she scrubbed and scrubbed, but the potatoes were again dirty when they came to the table.

The Dumonts' daughter Gertrude, who liked Isabella, did not want to see her continually being scolded, so she offered to help Isabella with the potatoes. Isabella scrubbed the potatoes as usual and put them in the pot to boil, then went to milk the cows. While she was gone, a hired servant Kate sneaked into the kitchen and dumped ashes into the potato water. She didn't know Gerty was watching. Gerty loudly proclaimed Isabella's innocence, and her good name was restored.

Isabella worked hard, often going without sleep, to please her master. Her fellow slaves were annoyed with her, saying all her hard work would do her no good, and only made the rest of them look bad. As a consequence, she developed no friendships with the other slaves.

She did, however, make friends with a young man from a neighboring farm named Bob. Bob's owner did not want his slave fathering children with someone else's female, so he forbade Bob to see Isabella. One day Isabella was very ill. Mr. Dumont came to her, asking if she had seen Bob. His owner was looking for him and was furious. Isabella said she had not seen him, but he very soon appeared on Dumont's land. His owner was not far behind. He and his son began beating Bob severely. Dumont ran them off, saying he would not have a slave killed on his property. Then he followed them home to be sure Bob was not killed. Bob was forced into marriage with one of his owner's slaves, but he soon died from his injuries.

Isabella had witnessed the beating from her sick bed. She heard Bob cry on the name of Jesus as he was being beaten. She had never heard the name before and wondered who He was and how He could help Bob.[31]

As a female slave, it is very likely that Isabella suffered sexual abuse. Her narrative, which she told to Olive Gilbert, says that certain episodes in her life are left out, for the sake of "decency." Some accuse Mr. Dumont of sexually abusing her, even suggesting he fathered one of her children,[32] while others claim Mrs. Dumont was the abuser.[33] In any event, Isabella was soon forced into marriage with an older slave named Tom. She and Tom had five children.

The State of New York passed a law that all slaves over the age of 40 were to be freed. Those under 40 were to be freed ten years later on July 4, 1827. Isabella took this happy news to her father, whom she had rarely been able to visit. Isabella's mother had died shortly after gaining her freedom, leaving Baumfree alone. The Hardenberghs had freed another aging couple, on the condition that they look after Baumfree. They were scarcely able to look after themselves, and died before Baumfree did. Isabella urged her father to hang on for ten more years until she could be free. She would care for her father, she said. Poor Baumfree longed for death. He knew he couldn't live another ten years. He died all alone in a cabin he had been given. There was not a morsel of food in the house.

Two years before the emancipation date, Mr. Dumont promised Isabella that, if she worked very hard, he would set her free one year early. Isabella worked as hard as ever, but she injured her hand. In spite of her injury, she continued to do as much work as before, but when the day came for her to be free,

Mr. Dumont reneged on his promise. He claimed her injury as his excuse, but Isabella knew she had not lacked in her duties. She believed she was free by Mr. Dumont's promise, but she decided to stay until the spinning was done, then she would leave.

Isabella was unsure how to go about leaving. She didn't want to run away in the night, since she did not consider herself a fugitive, but neither did she want to go by day, knowing she wouldn't get very far. She prayed and it seemed the answer came – leave at dawn before anyone was up. She also decided she would not go far, knowing Mr. Dumont would come looking for her and not wanting to put him out too much.

Isabella packed up her youngest child Sophie, leaving the rest behind, and left. She didn't know where to go, so she went to the home of someone she knew. He was dying, but he told her of two possible places she could find refuge. She went to the first one, which turned out to be the home of the Van Wageners. They were Christians and they happily took her in. When Mr. Dumont came looking for her, Mr. Van Wagener paid him off, giving him $20 for Isabella's services for the rest of the year, and another $5 for the baby. However, Mr. Van Wagener insisted he was not her master. Only one master ruled their household, the Lord Jesus Christ.

Under the New York law, slave children must continue to serve their masters until they were 25 for females and 28 for males.[34] It was illegal for slaves to be sold out of state, where they might never be freed. Mr. Dumont sold Isabella's son Peter to a Mr. Gedney of New York. Mr. Gedney wanted to take the boy to England with him, but soon found he was too small for the purpose, so he gave him to his brother Solomon Gedney. Solomon gave him to his sister Eliza's new husband, Mr. Fowler of Alabama. The Fowlers returned to Alabama, taking Peter with them.

When Isabella learned of this, and knowing that the

transaction was illegal, she went to see the Dumonts, demanding that her child be returned. Mrs. Dumont was totally unsympathetic and upbraided her for making "such a fuss over a little nigger." Isabella insisted she would get her child back. She then went to see Mrs. Gedney, Solomon's mother. Mrs. Gedney also treated her with disdain, insisting that if Alabama was good enough for her child Eliza, it was good enough for Isabella's child. Isabella pointed out that Eliza was a bride, not a slave. Isabella knew in her heart that God would help her.

Some Quaker friends suggested Isabella go to the courthouse and take her complaint to the grand jury. She had no clue what a grand jury was, so she approached the grandest looking man in the courthouse and began her complaint. He helped direct her to where she needed to go. As she once again made her complaint, a lawyer took her aside into another room. He asked her to swear on a Bible that the child in question was her son, which she did. He then gave her a writ to take to the constable in the town of New Paltz, asking him to serve it on Solomon Gedney. The constable unwittingly served the paper on Solomon's brother. Solomon fled, but on the advice of a lawyer, he went to Alabama to bring the child home.

When he returned, he had to post $600 bond against fleeing. The court would meet in a few months. Isabella was told she would have to wait. This she refused to do. She insisted they settle the matter right then, but the court date would not be changed.

Outside the courthouse, she met a man who inquired after her case. When she told him the situation he suggested she go to another lawyer who could help her. This lawyer agreed to help, but he needed $5 for expenses. She had no money, but returned to her Quaker friends. They gave her more than $5, every penny of which she passed on to the lawyer. He promised her she would have her son in 24 hours.

The next day Solomon Gedney produced the boy, who

pitched a fit, claiming Isabella was not his mother. He was so happy to be removed from the Fowlers that he feared a new situation, and so he begged to be allowed to stay with Gedney. The court believed Isabella, however, and ordered that the boy be returned to his mother. Later, upon examining him, she discovered that his back was covered in scars. He told horrible tales of being whipped and beaten by Fowler, and how other slaves suffered worse than he had. Isabella, in her anger, cried out to God, asking Him to render unto them double for what they had done to her boy.

One day Isabella went to visit the Dumonts, where some of her children were still living. While she was there, a fellow named Fred Waring, who had testified against her in the case of her son, asked how she had been and if she wouldn't mind going to his house to help with the workload. Isabella was happy to go, hoping to be able to reconcile with her former adversaries. They were related to the Gedneys.

While she was there, someone came running in, saying that Eliza had been murdered by her husband and a letter had come telling of the deed. Mrs. Gedney came in and they all went upstairs. Isabella believed she heard a voice telling her to go up and listen, so she did. The letter told how Fowler had beaten her and torn out her windpipe. Mrs. Gedney completely lost her senses as a result of the tragedy. Isabella felt shame for having wished upon them double. She never wanted something so horrible to happen and she repented before the Lord.

Isabella's spiritual training had been woefully incomplete. From her mother's teaching, she thought God was a powerful man in the sky, to whom she had to shout to be heard. She believed God answered her prayers when she was able to pray, but thought she could only pray when she was off by herself somewhere so she could pray loudly. She often bargained with God, promising to be good if He would give her what she asked for, but she found it impossible to keep up her end of the bargain.

Early in her service to Mr. Dumont, she thought no one could be more powerful than he, so she thought maybe Mr. Dumont was God. In time she learned that he was just a man, no better than anyone else.

Isabella had been taught to call on God in times of trouble, but when things were going well, she forgot about God. Once she had her freedom and had her son back, she felt no need for God.

Just like the Israelites as they wandered in the wilderness for 40 years, Isabella began to think she had been better off as a slave, working for Mr. Dumont. The holiday known to the Dutch as Pingster (Whitsuntide in English) was coming up. It was a time of great revelry among the slaves and Isabella wanted to be part of it. She announced to the Van Wageners that Mr. Dumont would be there to get her that day and that she would return with him. He arrived just as she had predicted but said he would not take her back. She believed he was joking and went to get her baby.

As she headed toward Mr. Dumont's wagon, she had a blinding vision of Almighty God barring the way. She discovered for the first time that He is omnipresent, omnipotent, and omniscient. She saw His holiness and her own sinfulness and she was shaken to the core. Mr. Dumont left and Isabella tried to return to her duties, but she couldn't. She knew she needed to get right with God without delay, but she was terrified to approach Him as she was. She needed an advocate to go between her and God. At that point, she received another vision, as the desired Advocate appeared.

She saw the beauty of His holiness and the enormity of His love for her, but she didn't know His name. In her soul she sensed that she knew Him, that she had always known Him, but at the same time she didn't know Him at all. Finally the words came to her mind, "It is Jesus." She welcomed Him into her heart as the best friend she had ever had. Still, she had much to learn. She guarded her relationship with Jesus jealously and was surprised to learn that others knew Him too.

Isabella and Peter moved to New York. Peter, throughout his growing up years, was frequently in trouble. Isabella had managed to get him a place in a school, but he was soon expelled for truancy. He began getting in trouble with the law. Isabella would bail him out, but finally realized she was not helping him. He would have to face his punishment. Eventually he was sent to sea on a whaling vessel. Isabella received letters from him periodically for a few years, but never saw him again.

In New York, Isabella lived with the Latourettes as a servant. Mrs. Latourette, with Isabella and other ladies, would go to the red light district and minister to the women they found there.

Through her acquaintance with the Latourettes, Isabella met Elijah Pierson and eventually became his housekeeper. Mr. Pierson declared himself to be the prophet Elijah the Tishbite[35] He became acquainted with Robert Matthews, who called himself Matthias. The first time Matthias showed up at their doorstep, Isabella was home alone. She thought he looked like Jesus and was well impressed with him.

Matthias declared himself to be God on earth. He said the spirit of God the Father was upon him, and he called Pierson John the Baptist. He preached that there is no heaven except on earth and there is no resurrection, only reincarnation. The spirits of dead saints inhabit the present generation.

Matthias proclaimed that he was ushering in the kingdom of God on earth. Isabella, Mr. Pierson, and several other followers all moved into a house they called Zion Hill to live communally and spread the kingdom. All were supposed to work for the good of the community, but it soon seemed as though Isabella was doing most of the work.

Some of the other residents of the house were a widow

named Catherine Galloway and a married couple named Ben and Ann Folger, as well as the Folgers' son Edward and Mr. Pierson's daughter Elizabeth.

Matthias was now being called "Father" by the residents. Mrs. Folger seemed overly anxious to please him. When Mr. Folger went to New York on business, Mrs. Folger flirted outrageously with Matthias. Matthias came to the conclusion and began to preach that only God could choose perfect mates for men and women, whom he called "match spirits." He declared that Mrs. Folger was indeed his match spirit, and Mr. Folger would just have to give her up and be happy about it. A wedding ceremony was held where Mr. Folger actually handed his wife over to Matthias. Mrs. Folger then took the title "Mother."

Life in the "kingdom" continued to get more and more seedy. Matthias sent for his children from his "previous" marriage. One was an 18-year-old daughter who, upon arrival, told her father she was married. He whipped her soundly, declared her marriage annulled and performed a marriage ceremony between her and Ben Folger. Catherine Galloway was most upset over this because she had been having an affair with Ben.

Isabella knew she had been duped. Once again she had believed that a mortal man might be God. When she realized her mistake, she wanted to leave, but she was afraid the children might be harmed, so she stayed. She knew God was not speaking through Matthias, but she also knew He was no longer speaking to her either. By this time, Matthias had banned prayer among the community.

Rumors of the goings on at Zion Hill spread throughout the town. The townspeople wanted to drive them all away, but they no doubt enjoyed the gossip as well.

One day, Matthias' daughter's husband showed up with a deputy, who demanded that she be returned to her lawful husband. With her departure, Ben resumed his relationship with Catherine, but eventually he began demanding his own wife back. For a while, Ann bounced between the two men.

Mr. Pierson fell ill, having occasional fits. One day, after over-indulging in under-ripe blackberries, he had a massive fit, which left him unable to rise and care for himself. Isabella and Elizabeth tended him, but a week later he died.

The Folgers signed a deposition that implied that Matthias and Isabella killed Pierson with poison and attempted to kill the Folgers. Armed with letters of reference to her honesty from former employers and Mr. Dumont, Isabella sued the Folgers for slander.

Before her suit came to trial, Matthias was tried for murder, but was acquitted due to lack of evidence. The Folgers had recanted their slanderous comments about Isabella, but she would not withdraw her suit. She won the case and was awarded $125.[36]

Isabella continued to work as a servant wherever she could find work. It seemed she worked hard and never could get ahead. One day it occurred to her that she had been miserly, snatching up every opportunity to earn a coin and depriving others who needed the work as badly as herself. In shame over her actions she adopted a new attitude towards money.

Shortly after that, on June 1, 1843, she decided to begin her life as a sojourner, traveling east from New York. She told her employer that her name was no longer Isabella, but Sojourner. When asked why she was going she replied, "The Spirit calls me there, and I must go."[37] Later, when she asked the Lord for a second name, He gave her the word "Truth." She found that to be a fitting name. As a slave she had always held the name of her master. Now she would be working solely for the Lord, who is the Truth.

Her message as she traveled was to exhort people to embrace Jesus and refrain from sin. Sometimes she joined others' meetings, sometimes she held her own, with large crowds. Sometimes she would stay in one place for a few days and work to replenish her funds and her energy, but then she would move on.

To study the Bible, she had children read it to her rather than adults, because the children would not offer a commentary on the text, as the adults would invariably do. Also, the children would happily repeat a verse over and over again if Sojourner asked them to.

She met up with adherents of the Second Advent doctrines, those who were eagerly expecting the Second Coming of Christ and the pre-tribulation rapture of the church. After listening to their beliefs, she expounded her own. She was appalled at the idea of the Christians being removed while the wicked were burned up, and then returning to walk on the ashes of the wicked. She declared that if the Lord came to burn up the wicked, she intended to stay right there in the midst of the fire, like Shadrach, Meshach, and Abednego, protected by Jesus from the flames. She shouted, "Do you tell me that God's children *can't stand fire?*"[38]

One time at a camp meeting in Northampton, a mob of rowdy young men threatened to break up the meeting and to burn the tent. Everyone, including Sojourner, was terrified. She, as the only black person present, feared being accosted more violently than the rest and hid in a corner. Then, in shame over her cowardice, she proclaimed to herself, "Shall I run away and hide from the Devil? Me, a servant of the living God? Have I not faith enough to go out and quell that mob, when I know it is written – 'One shall chase a thousand, and two put ten thousand to flight'? I know there are not a thousand here; and I know I am a servant of the living God. I'll go to the rescue, and the Lord shall go with and protect me."[39]

She invited another to go with her, but was refused, so she went alone to a knoll and sang her favorite hymn very loudly.

The young men gathered around her and asked her to sing to them again, or preach, or pray. She preached and sang to them for an hour, but they showed no sign of leaving. Finally, she pointed out to them that she had honored their request and now they must honor hers. She would sing one more song, and then they must leave. She wouldn't begin until she got them all to promise to leave. She sang the hymn and the crowd left. Some were still bent on mischief, but their fellows would not allow them to break their word to the old woman.

In Northampton, Sojourner attached herself to another group of people living in community. They called themselves the Northampton Association of Education and Industry.[40] They produced silk and held everything in common. They loved debating new ideas and theological issues. Although they differed widely on religion, they were held together by their common contempt for slavery.

While there, Sojourner met William Lloyd Garrison and Frederick Douglass. The only other black person there was David Ruggles, an old, blind man who had worked for the underground railroad. He was dearly loved by the children, who fought to be near him and to help him.

Sojourner also met Olive Gilbert in the Association, who later wrote her autobiography, *Narrative of Sojourner Truth*, for her. Peddling her books became her chief source of income when Sojourner had returned to wandering, after the collapse of the Association.

At one time some friends gave Sojourner a horse and buggy for her travels. Sometimes she would come to a crossroad and wouldn't know which way to go. She would drop the reins and say, "God, you drive."[41]

Isabella became a well-known speaker in abolitionist circles, but she also spoke out on women's rights. She attended the first National Woman's Rights Convention. As the only black woman there, she at first couldn't identify with the other women and their complaint, but as the convention went on, she began to see the similarities in the injustices they had all suffered. Although the newspapers referred to it as a Hen Convention, many of Sojourner's abolitionist male friends were there, including Garrison and Douglass.

At one speaking engagement, Sojourner was accused of speaking against the Constitution. She replied:

> Children, I talks to God, and God talks to me. I goes out and talks to God in the fields and in the woods. This morning I was walking out, and I got over the fence. I saw the wheat a-holding up its head, looking very big. I goes up and takes a-hold of it. You believe it, there was no wheat there? I says, 'God, what *is* the matter with this wheat?' and he says to me, 'Sojourner, there is a little weasel [weevil] in it.' Now I hears talking about the Constitution and the rights of man. I comes up and I takes hold of this Constitution. It looks mighty big, and I feels for *my* rights, but there aren't any there. Then I says, 'God, what *ails* this Constitution?' He says to me, 'Sojourner, there is a little weasel in it.'[42]

Life had become more difficult for blacks in the North. A Fugitive Slave Law was passed to appease the South. Any black person could be arrested on the word of two witnesses and sent into slavery without due process, whether or not he or she was a runaway.[43]

Fevers ran so high in the nation over the slavery issue that a southern Congressman beat an abolitionist Senator right in the Senate chambers. John Brown was also going around inciting violence against pro-slavery men. It was at this time that Frederick Douglass began calling for blacks to rise up and take their freedom by force.

Sojourner, who had never believed in resorting to violence, sat quietly listening to Douglass' speech. Then she spoke up and said, "Douglass, is God dead?"[44] Her simple question changed the tenor of the meeting.

Sojourner continued traveling about, preaching her message about when she found Jesus, and speaking against slavery. She was once a guest in the home of Harriet Beecher Stowe, the author of *Uncle Tom's Cabin.*

She traveled through Ohio and Indiana. In Indiana a rumor started that she was a man in woman's clothing. They demanded that she expose her breasts to some of the ladies present, who would verify her gender. Sojourner opened her dress and exposed her breasts for the whole crowd to see, saying, "It is not my shame but yours that I do this."[45]

When Civil War broke out, Sojourner retired to a home she had bought in Battle Creek, Michigan. There she was able to gather together some of her daughters and grandchildren. One grandson, James Caldwell, enlisted in the first black regiment and went off to fight. He was captured in battle and held prisoner until the end of the war, when he returned home safely.

Sojourner helped with the war effort. She learned that several of the black youth from Battle Creek who had joined the army were camped in Detroit. She solicited donations to take them a Thanksgiving dinner. Most people gladly gave a donation, all except one fellow who refused with a rude comment about the war and the "niggers." Sojourner asked, "Who are you?"

"I'm the only son of my mother," was his answer.

"I'm glad there's no more," Sojourner said.[46]

Sojourner joined with another abolitionist, Josephine Griffing, during the war, to go and speak throughout Indiana. Indiana had passed a law making it illegal for Negroes to enter the state. Sojourner was immediately arrested, but when her companion argued with the judge that the law was unconstitutional, he ordered that Sojourner be freed.[47]

Throughout Indiana, hecklers shouted so loudly they disrupted the meetings. Union soldiers were called upon to take Sojourner into custody for her own protection, yet she continued to speak.

She traveled to Washington DC and saw the terrible conditions of freed slaves in the city. They had no work and lived in squalor.

Sojourner was able to obtain an audience with President Lincoln. He signed the book she carried, which she called her Book of Life.

She went to work in Freedman's Village in Washington, teaching the women how to take care of their homes and children. The women had formerly been field hands and had no experience with housework. Sojourner also taught the women to stand up for their rights. Marauders from Maryland would come and steal children away. The mothers felt powerless to stop it until Sojourner told them the law was on their side. The next group of child-stealers found mothers ready to fight with their bare hands to protect their children.[48]

Sojourner then went to work at Freedman's Hospital, which was full of war wounded. She taught the nurses how to make beds, clean wounds, and change bandages. On Sundays she preached the gospel to the patients.

Her work at the hospital required that she ride the streetcars once in a while. This proved to be another battleground for Sojourner. The city of Washington DC had done away with Jim Crow cars, allowing any passenger to sit where he pleased. As a result, however, many streetcar drivers refused to stop and pick up black people. Sojourner one day shouted so loudly, "I want to ride, I want to ride!" that she created a traffic jam. The streetcar was forced to stop, so Sojourner hopped on, in spite of the driver's threats.

She often had to fight for her right to ride, and even bear the brunt of insulting remarks from other passengers. One day a conductor shoved her so roughly he dislocated her shoulder. She sued for assault and battery, and the conductor lost his job. After that, black people had considerably less trouble getting rides on streetcars.

After the war, Sojourner struggled to find employment for the freed slaves in Washington, but there were too many for her to even make a dent. She decided that the best thing to do for them was to get Congress to grant them land out west, where they could work and be productive citizens.

In order for Congress to hear her, she needed many signatures on a petition. For the next several years she traveled the country speaking and filling the petition with signatures. Just when she was ready to present the petition, her grandson and traveling companion, Sammy, fell ill. She returned with him to Michigan, but he died. Sojourner herself became very ill and was rumored, for the second time, to have died. But she was miraculously restored to health. She believed the Lord raised her up so she could continue her work.

However, Congress was no longer interested in helping the former slaves. Sojourner knew it would be useless to present her petition at that time. She turned instead to speaking out on other social issues, such as women's rights, prison reform, temperance, and capital punishment.

Speaking on women's rights one time she said, "I am sometimes told that 'women ain't fit to vote, why, don't you know that a woman had seven devils in her: and do you suppose a woman is fit to rule the nation?' Seven devils ain't no account; a man had a legion in him. The devils didn't know where to go; and so they asked that they might go into the swine. They thought that was as good a place as they came out from."[49] She considered it just plain meanness to withhold rights from women.

Then in 1877 she noticed that many black singles and

families had begun moving to Kansas on their own. With little protection from the government, their lives were in danger in the deep South, so many left to seek their fortunes elsewhere.[50] To Sojourner, it was clearly the hand of God, completing a task that was just too big for an old woman alone.

She was able to make a trip to Kansas to see the phenomenon for herself before returning home to Battle Creek. She died there November 26, 1883, surrounded by her daughters and their families.

Laura Haviland, one of Sojourner's companions in the anti-slavery fight, wrote in her diary for her young son's future reading, "She [Sojourner] has a superior mind, and her abiding faith in God is beautiful. She talks of Him and to Him as familiarly as your father and I talk to each other."[51]

In her life, Sojourner was sometimes led astray by false teaching, but when she learned to hear the voice of God and allowed Him to be her teacher, she was able to serve Him with her whole heart. She was illiterate, yet many people marveled over her understanding of the Scriptures and theology.

When Christ came into her heart, she was filled with such love that she swore she could love even the white folks. Indeed, she spent much of her career working among white people. She was afraid they would suffer the wrath of God if they did not repent and rid themselves of slavery. Her name was well known among the white majority, but few blacks had ever heard of her.

Sojourner didn't live to see all of the causes for which she fought come to fruition. I'm sure she would have been filled with sorrow to know that one hundred years after the Civil War, black people would still have to fight for their right to ride public transportation. But Sojourner believed in the law and she feared only God. Woe be unto anyone who violated her rights under the law.

In many ways she was a woman ahead of her time. She knew God loved her and that God is no respecter of persons. In

God's eyes, she was no better or worse than anyone else on the planet. With God's help, there was nothing she couldn't accomplish.

Aimee Semple McPherson

"But you shall receive power when the Holy Spirit has come upon you; and you shall be My witnesses both in Jerusalem, and in all Judea and Samaria, and even to the remotest part of the earth."
– Acts 1: 8

"Blessed are you when men cast insults at you, and persecute you, and say all kinds of evil against you falsely, on account of Me. Rejoice, and be glad, for your reward in heaven is great, for so they persecuted the prophets who were before you."
– Matthew 5: 11-12

If ever there was a woman anointed to preach the gospel of Jesus Christ, that woman was Aimee Semple McPherson. When she preached she packed whatever building they were in and people were healed in numbers that very likely had not been seen since the end of the Apostolic Age. The anointing was so strong that, fifty-five years after her death, as I read her book *This is That*, I could scarcely read a few pages without having to stop and praise the Lord for the mighty works He had wrought through this woman.

Aimee's life was not without controversy. She was divorced twice, dragged into court on more than one occasion, and was at the center of several scandals. No doubt she came under severe spiritual attack because she ardently stormed the gates of hell. She took Jesus at His word when he said "Go!" and she went into the places few evangelists will venture, into red light districts and dance halls, ministering to prostitutes, drug addicts, and teenage mothers. She had a love for the lost that had to have come from the heart of the Savior Himself. Whatever else she was, Aimee Semple McPherson was a woman of God.

Aimee's mother Minnie, a devout Salvation Army member, had been orphaned at a young age. She went to live in the home of James Kennedy to care for his ailing wife, who died shortly thereafter. Minnie and James were married a few months later.

Minnie had sensed a call on her life to spread the gospel, but believed her marital responsibilities precluded her fulfillment of that call. Consequently, she went to her knees and asked the Lord to grant her a girl child whom she would send in her place to preach the gospel. The Lord answered her prayer and Aimee Elizabeth was born on Oct. 9, 1890 near a small town in Canada. When the baby was six weeks old, Minnie bundled her up and took her to the Salvation Army meeting to dedicate her to the Lord.

Aimee's upbringing was steeped in religious training. She participated in her mother's Salvation Army meetings, as well as her father's Methodist church. However, "higher criticism" was at its height in those days, with its teachings that the Bible was not entirely accurate in everything that it said. Also, it was commonly taught that the age of miracles had ended long ago. As a consequence, when Aimee, as a teenager, encountered secular teachings on the theory of evolution, her faith was shaken to the core. If the Bible was not to be believed in certain areas, how could she believe it in anything? How did she even know there was a God?

She began asking questions of church leaders, the pastor, and her mother, but received no satisfactory answers. To her mother's horror, she became an outspoken critic of religion. One day a Pentecostal evangelistic meeting took place in her town. She persuaded her father to take her, mostly out of curiosity. The evangelist, Robert Semple, preached on the need for repentance and Aimee was convicted. Some say she was moved as much by her attraction to the evangelist himself as she was by his stirring words. Regardless, her conversion was genuine.

Aimee devoted herself to Bible study and seeking the baptism of the Holy Spirit with such fervor that it became her whole focus. She could no longer attend to her schoolwork, so her grades began to fall and she was in danger of failing. In addition, her mother's Salvation Army associates claimed Aimee was setting a poor example for other young people. Her mother laid down the law, forcing Aimee to choose between Pentecostal meetings and school. The next day, on her way to school, she stopped at the home of her Pentecostal friends to pray over the matter and ended up staying there all day. When it came time to go home, she discovered that she was snowed in, so she happily stayed where she was.

She continued seeking the Holy Ghost. On the following Saturday morning, she got up before everyone else and began again to pray and plead with God. Then she heard the Lord say, "Now, child, cease your strivings and your begging; just begin to praise Me, and in simple, child-like faith, receive ye the Holy Ghost." She began saying "Glory to Jesus" until she finally burst forth in praises in a language she had never learned and she was awash in the glory and majesty of God.[52]

When the snowstorm ended, Aimee returned home to another storm, this one from her mother, who forbade her to have anything more to do with the Pentecostals. In desperation, Aimee challenged her mother to prove to her from the Bible that the Pentecostals were wrong. Minnie eagerly took up the challenge. Many hours of Bible study later, Minnie could only conclude that Pentecostal teachings were indeed in line with the Scriptures.

Robert Semple, who had been present the day Aimee received the baptism of the Holy Spirit, asked for her hand in marriage. They were married August 12, 1908. The following January, Robert was ordained by William Durham at Full Gospel Assembly in Chicago.[53] Later, Aimee was also ordained.

The young couple busied themselves in evangelistic meetings. One day Aimee fell down a flight of stairs and dislocated her ankle, twisting the foot completely backwards. The foot was set in a cast and Aimee was told to stay off of it for five weeks. It was swollen and black and blue, and so painful Aimee could barely get around with crutches. One week after the accident Aimee believed the Lord had told her to take her shoe and go to the mission center where their close associate William Durham was preaching. In obedience, she wrapped up her shoe and hobbled to the meeting. The pain was so great she needed to be carried the last few feet. At the meeting, Brother Durham laid his hand on her foot and prayed. She said the pain immediately left her. She insisted the cast be removed, which it was, and to everyone's amazement, her shoe fit perfectly and she was able to walk normally. From that moment on, Aimee knew for certain that God still heals people today, just as He did years ago.

Robert Semple believed they were being called to China to serve as missionaries, so in 1910 they set sail for the Far East, traveling first to Ireland to visit Robert's family. While in Ireland, Aimee discovered she was expecting their first child.

Arriving in Asia, they settled in Hong Kong, but things did not go well from the start. Both of them became very sick with malaria and had to be hospitalized. Aimee gradually regained her strength, but Robert never did. He died on August 19, 1910, one month before his daughter Roberta was born. In sorrow, Aimee returned home with her tiny infant.

She moved to New York, where her mother was engaged in Salvation Army work among new immigrants. Shortly after that she went home to Canada to stay with her aged father. Aimee was trying to get back into evangelistic work, but Roberta was not a healthy child and needed her mother's attention. Aimee then returned to New York, so her mother could help with Roberta.

Aimee began seeing Harold McPherson in 1911. They loved to visit the theatre. Many of the fascinating scenes and special effects Aimee saw there later worked their way into her services.[54]

Aimee and Harold were married Feb. 5, 1912 and moved to Chicago. Aimee's friends in Chicago encouraged her to get back into church work, much to Harold's dismay. He wanted an ordinary housewife, not a public Christian servant. He moved the family to Providence, Rhode Island. Their son Rolf was born March 23, 1913.

Aimee did her best to be a good housewife and mother, but she felt like she was neglecting her call. She suffered bouts of depression, and eventually became so sick she was hospitalized. She had a hysterectomy, but showed no signs of improvement. In fact she grew worse and the doctors despaired of her life. She was put in a room for the dying.

As she lay near death, she believed the Lord spoke to her saying, "Now will you go?" She replied aloud that she would go. Those around her bedside supposed she was leaving this world, but instead she began to recover.

Once back on her feet, she was determined that she would not fail God again. She told Harold of her decision to work for God, but he was less than enthusiastic, so one day she packed up her children and left him. She later sent him a note, inviting him to join her, but he refused and insisted that she come home. This she could not do, for she had once again put her hand to the plow and could not turn back. She believed God had forgiven her for walking away from His will and had anointed her afresh with His Holy Spirit.

Her first invitation to lead a crusade came from a woman

who had started a church in Mt. Forest, Canada. Aimee was soon drawing large crowds. One night her husband showed up. He had come to bring her home, but when he heard her preach, he knew she would never go back to being a housewife. He went to the altar and received the baptism of the Holy Spirit. Aimee was overjoyed, believing that together they could spread the gospel. Indeed, it was Harold's aim to do just that. However, his commitment often wavered. They had children to feed, and evangelistic work was uncertain. He took a job, but experienced dreams where he believed God was telling him to leave his job and help Aimee with her work.

They went on the road, traveling as far south as Florida. Harold took care of the logistics, finding spots for their tent and getting everything set up, while Aimee led the services. He would sometimes hear others referring to himself as "only the preacher's husband,"[55] which did nothing for his self-esteem.

They continued to travel up and down the east coast, taking Rolf with them, but leaving Roberta with Minnie, because of her frail health. Sometimes they would stop and preach to people working in the fields.

Aimee reluctantly gave in to social customs of the day in the south and held separate meetings for blacks and whites. But in Key West, the segregation broke down when curious whites came to the meeting set up for blacks. For the first time ever in Key West, blacks and whites worshipped under the same roof.[56]

Early in 1918, Aimee and Harold separated. He attempted to work as an evangelist himself, but had very little success. He eventually quit and returned to secular work. Aimee's mother Minnie joined her, caring for the children and overseeing the administrative details. Her help was invaluable to Aimee and continued for many years.

In 1921 Harold quietly divorced her. Their parting was amicable, but put a black mark on her ministry. Critics, already opposed to her ministry because of her gender, used her divorce against her. She maintained that her commitment to God was more important than social conventions, and she must be about the Lord's work. She and her mother and children headed west, becoming, quite possibly, the first women on their own to cross the United States by automobile.

It was a long journey, as they averaged about a hundred miles a day. Sometimes the wheels would get stuck in the mud and Aimee would have to get out and push. Along the way they held evangelistic meetings in order to raise funds to keep going. Also, they had signs on the "gospel car" which read "Jesus is Coming Soon – Get Ready" and "Where will you spend eternity?" These signs created quite a stir wherever they went. Apparently these were things people had not considered before, so they flocked to the car to get literature, which was handed out in abundance.

One high point of the trip for Aimee came in Indianapolis, where they stopped long enough to meet and worship with Maria Woodworth-Etter, another popular female evangelist.

Eventually the women and children arrived in Los Angeles, which became their headquarters and home. Aimee soon had a large following in Los Angeles, but she didn't stay put. She found herself crossing the U.S. many times in the next few years, preaching now here and now there. Everywhere she went she packed the house, though sometimes she had to go out and beat the bushes herself. For example, in Winnipeg, her suggestion to church members that they invite non-churched persons to the meetings was met with blank stares, so she took it upon herself to issue the invitations. She went to the red light district and to dance halls, demonstrating love and acceptance to the people, who then turned up in droves to her meetings.

There were massive campaigns in St. Louis, Denver, San Jose, and San Diego, as well as many other cities throughout the United States and Canada. The power of God so filled the meeting halls that many people were unable to remain on their feet in God's presence. Indeed, when Aimee traveled to San Jose in March 1921, people totally unconnected to the revival meetings reported being "slain in the spirit" in their own homes, knocked down flat and speaking in tongues.[57]

In the early days, one fellow who didn't believe religion needed to be a thing of the heart, received the baptism and shouted praise to God in tongues. He wondered if he'd ever be able to speak English again. Sister Aimee wrote, "Sometimes the greatest doubters get the biggest baptisms and the people who despise making noise make the most noise of all when they receive this old-time power."[58]

Physical healings became a large part of her services in the early years, so that she would often hold separate healing services. In San Diego, the services were so big, and so many were being turned away, that the decision was made to hold a healing service outdoors, where more people could come. Even so, the multitude of people who wanted prayer for healing was more than one woman could touch. Her heart broke when she looked on the sea of hurting humanity, knowing she would be unable to pray for each one individually. Yet she would stay and work until she was exhausted and was pulled away from the crowd by her helpers.

This was often the case, as day after day Aimee would strive to touch and pray for as many people as possible. Some people were healed while they waited in line or while they prayed themselves, with never a touch from Sister McPherson, but the vast majority were only healed after being personally ministered to.

Aimee's mother Minnie also worked tirelessly, sometimes getting only two hours rest each night. She would go very early in the morning to pray with people as they waited for the doors to open and giving healing cards to those who needed them so they could get in line. Some were healed when Minnie prayed for them.

In San Francisco, local ministers offered to pray for the sick, relieving Aimee of the burden. Over 700 were prayed for in two days and many received healing, even though Aimee herself was not present.[59]

Aimee's own claims were that most of the people who were prayed for received healing, in some cases even as many as eighty percent.[60] She attributed the non-healings to lack of faith on the part of the seeker and an unwillingness to do for themselves, expecting Aimee's faith to be sufficient for them.

Newspaper clippings also documented a staggering number of healings. Even the American Medical Association of San Francisco went to her meetings to see for themselves. They reported that the healings were "genuine, beneficial and wonderful."[61]

There were many, many testimonies from those who were healed from all manner of illnesses. The blind saw, the lame walked, the deaf heard, and the poor had the gospel preached to them. Harriet Jordan gave the following testimony:

She had been born with an intestinal disorder that left her a sickly child, and yet she grew to adulthood. As a young adult her intestines pressed on her stomach, causing ulcers. She had surgery, but then her intestines fused together and became covered with adhesions. More surgery would remove the adhesions and separate the intestines, but they would quickly grow together again. After seven surgeries, her doctor said there was nothing more they could do. She was in constant and severe pain, relieved only by opiates.

Harriet trusted in Jesus, though, and began searching the scriptures for evidence of divine healing, wondering why no one preached on healing. When she heard of Aimee Semple McPherson, she determined to go see her. Her nurse and sister practically carried her there. She prayed throughout the service, promising to serve the Lord if she was healed. When she was taken to the stage, she was surrounded by a brilliant light, which was not visible to others. She knew she was in the presence of the Lord. Aimee prayed, but Harriet could scarcely hear her, so caught up was she with the Lord. Others later told her that she ran off the stage and shouted in her joy. She remained for three days in the glory of the Lord and then gave her life to serving Him, teaching Sunday school and working at Angelus Temple.[62]

Aimee's primary concern was the salvation of souls, so she downplayed her role as a healing evangelist. Yet many people did receive physical healing. A follow-up from one crusade showed that ninety percent of those who claimed healing said they were still healed a few weeks later.[63] Aimee herself believed the scriptures, where they told of Jesus' healing ministry, and she held fast to *Hebrews 13: 8*, which says, "Jesus Christ is the same yesterday and today, *yes* and forever." Since Jesus healed yesterday, it is only natural that He should continue to heal today. Her faith in Jesus' love and power never wavered.

Aimee also fervently believed in the power of prayer. One time when she was about to preach in Kansas, it began to pour down rain, just as the service was about to begin. Although they had been wet before, Aimee was afraid the people would not be able to hear the message, so she quickly jumped to her feet and prayed:

> Oh Lord, stay this rain and this storm. You can just hold it in the hollow of your hand. Lord, don't you see these people have come these many miles and don't you see we have come these many miles to preach this word to them. We don't mind going home in the rain, dear Lord, but if it is Thy will stay it and if the land hath need of it, let it fall after the message has been delivered to these hungry souls.[64]

The rain immediately stopped and the sun came out.

In Los Angeles, people had donated land, time, and materials to build a house for Aimee and her children, so the children could grow up in a more stable environment than they had previously known.

Next came the construction of Angelus Temple in Echo Park, which would seat more than five thousand. Aimee chose for its setting a beautiful park, so that those who waited for hours to gain admittance to a meeting could wait in a pleasant environment, where they could picnic if they chose. It officially opened January 1, 1923.

Aimee had a creative mind for publicity. As a way of drawing attention to the newly opened Temple, she entered a float, shaped like the Temple, in the Tournament of Roses parade, and even took a prize for the float.

Services were held every day at the Temple. One service each week would be especially for children and one would be a healing service. Aimee soon became famous for her "illustrated sermons," which incorporated drama into the sermon. She wrote all these herself. In many ways she was ahead of her time, as many seeker-oriented churches today also use drama and contemporary music to attract the unchurched.

Aimee preached a simple message of salvation in Christ, emphasizing *Hebrews 13: 8*. She never threatened people with hell, but persuaded them with the love of Christ, which she amply evidenced by loving them herself. She used the colorful illustrations to make her point and used simple language that the people could understand.

Her foursquare gospel had taken shape in 1922 with Christ as the center, emphasizing Jesus, the Only Savior; Jesus, the Great Physician; Jesus, the Baptizer with the Holy Ghost; and Jesus, the Coming Bridegroom, Lord and King. The International Church of the Foursquare Gospel, the denomination that Aimee founded, continues to uphold these tenets today.

Music was a large part of her services and Aimee used songs that were well-known old favorites, as well as contemporary choruses. Her services were well organized and emotional, but without many of the loud excesses that often characterized Pentecostal meetings.

Aimee reached across denominational lines, which sometimes became a cause for criticism. She took what she had learned from her Methodist and Salvation Army upbringing, as well as her Pentecostal conversion, and wove them all together. She believed that salvation through Christ was offered freely to any who would receive it. In 1924, the Temple recorded 14,000 people giving their lives to Christ.[65]

Aimee used a follow-up method, which is similar to what many evangelists use today. She recorded the names and denominational association of the people who responded to her message. After she had left a particular city, the names would be given to local churches, so that they could contact the new converts and help them continue on their walk.

Aimee preached an inclusive gospel, believing that the blood of Christ was shed for all, rich and poor, black and white, male and female. She preached to black congregations as willingly as white. Yet in the early years of her ministry she received support and financial gifts from the Ku Klux Klan without speaking out against their racism. That changed in 1924. One night several hooded Klan members strode into the Temple. People in the front rows gave up their seats to the Klan. Aimee decided right then to change her sermon topic. She preached against the sin of racism, illustrating how un-Christlike those who practice it can be. As a body, the Klan members rose and left, but later men were seen coming back in the building one by one. The next day Echo Park, were the Temple stood, was littered with white robes.

The early years in Los Angeles were highly successful. In

1922 she became the first woman to preach a sermon on radio,[66] and she continued to broadcast regularly. She also started a training institute for evangelists and missionaries, which was called Lighthouse of International Foursquare Evangelism, or L.I.F.E. for short. In addition, Angelus Temple included a commissary, where food and clothing was handed out to any who needed it, without the red tape that often accompanied such requests. Other services to the community that the Temple offered were an employment bureau, parole committee, summer camps, and Bible conferences. Most importantly, the Temple included a prayer tower, which was staffed 24 hours a day, sending constant prayers toward heaven.

Of course, there were those who were skeptical at first. One man, Charles Price, thought the members of his Congregational Church had fallen under some sort of sickness after visiting Sister Aimee's meetings. When he went to investigate for himself, he eventually yielded and went to the altar seeking the baptism of the Holy Ghost. When he returned to his church he preached with a new vigor that drew large crowds. He then left his pastorate and traveled throughout America and Canada, preaching and healing as he went.[68]

Aimee's critics soon had a juicy piece of gossip to hold against her, when in May of 1926 she went to the beach for a swim and didn't return for six weeks. It was feared she had drowned, but no body washed up on the shore. In addition, rumors began circulating that she had been seen in a lovers' nest with a married man who had worked in her radio studio. The man in question made his presence known four weeks before Aimee reappeared, denying all allegations.

When Aimee was found, she claimed to have been kidnapped and held in a cabin in Mexico. She had escaped and walked many miles, until she was taken across the border into Texas and hospitalized. Aimee had been kidnapped before by the Ku Klux Klan and had been threatened by others in the months prior to her abduction, even by the Mob. (Many prostitutes, drug dealers, and others who worked for the Mob had been saved through Aimee's preaching. Besides giving up their former occupations, they were also going on the radio giving testimonies and were naming names).[69]

Still, there were parts of her story that did not seem to match the physical evidence. For example, her shoes were not scuffed from the long walk, nor did she show any signs of dehydration or sunburn, or even perspiration on her dress.[70] The police could not find the cabin she said she had been held in, nor did they ever find the kidnappers, even though Minnie had received a ransom note prior to Aimee's reappearance.

But there were holes in the lovers' tryst story as well. The prime witness changed her story several times and other witnesses' stories did not hold up under cross-examination. Some evidence disappeared and other pieces were eliminated by forensics.[71] Aimee and her mother were both charged with perjury, but the charges were later dropped due to lack of evidence. To this day, no satisfactory evidence has ever been produced to substantiate either story. One thing is for certain, though, and that is that Aimee never changed her story.

From that point on it seemed the press couldn't get enough of printing malicious gossip about Aimee. Her relationship with her mother came under scrutiny. Minnie was a very efficient businesswoman. She was in charge of the finances at Angelus Temple, and her strictness often offended many of the workers, who complained to Aimee. Eventually, Aimee asked for her mother's resignation, saying she would handle the business affairs herself. Administration was not her gifting, however, and after only a couple of years she asked her mother to come back. Minnie returned for a few months to straighten out the mess caused by corrupt and incompetent managers.

In the fall of 1930 Aimee suffered a nervous collapse. Struggling to regain her health, she took a trip with her daughter Roberta.

Many other controversies had arisen during those years. Some complained that she had become too materialistic. Also, there seemed to be constant bickering among Temple employees, leading to divisions. Some members who left returned a short time later.

But in September 1931, Aimee married for the third time. Because of her previous divorce, many found this marriage untenable and quit the Temple for good.

She continued to struggle with poor health in the early 1930s. In addition, her husband had been sued for breach of promise and was found liable. In 1933 he sued for divorce. Aimee publicly repented of her marriage, stating that it was wrong for a divorced person to remarry while their former spouse lived.

Aimee frequently found herself debating other notables. She debated Rev. Ben M. Bogard of the Antioch Missionary Baptist Church over the issue of healing. He had called her "the devil in skirts." The crowd at the debate was clearly on Aimee's side. The evening concluded with testimonies from three people who claimed to have been healed when Aimee prayed for them, and she was declared the winner of the debate.[72] Later, Charles Lee Smith of the American Association for the Advancement of Atheism challenged Aimee to debate him over the issue of evolution. She agreed, and once again was overwhelmingly declared the victor.[73]

Trouble was also brewing in Europe in the mid-1930s. Daniel Epstein writes that in 1935 Aimee "led the American clergy in a violent denunciation of Hitler and Mussolini from the pulpit. And she was among the first to defend the establishment of a Jewish homeland in Palestine."[74] She also spoke prophecies of impending trouble on August 3, 7 and September 28, the very same days that Hitler met with Mussolini to divide Europe.[75] Later, during the war, Aimee took an active part selling war bonds and sending Bibles and literature to the soldiers.

In 1936 Aimee and her daughter Roberta had a falling out. Roberta left the Temple and sued Aimee's lawyer for slander. For some unknown reason, Aimee took the lawyer's side, even though his competency had always been questionable.

Later, Aimee also had a falling out with her associate pastor Rheba Crawford. Crawford sued Aimee for slander, to the tune of one million dollars. When both sides recognized the shame of their actions, the suit was settled out of court.[76]

Trouble seemed to dog Aimee's footsteps in the latter years of her life and ministry. In 1936 Giles Knight became the assistant business manager of the Echo Park Evangelistic Association, and was later promoted to general manager. The affairs of Angelus Temple regained a measure of respectability after Knight took over. He ruled with an iron fist and got the Temple out of debt. He controlled where Aimee went and who she saw. It proved to be a great time for Aimee artistically, as she accomplished a lot during that time, but she was also terribly lonely. Knight would not allow Roberta to communicate with her mother, so they were never able to reconcile. In Feb. 1944 Knight resigned. Aimee's son Rolf McPherson was appointed vice president of the Echo Park Evangelistic Association, which he ably led until his retirement.

Aimee welcomed the freedom she regained with Knight's departure, but her health had deteriorated to such a state that she could not take advantage of her freedom. She died in a hotel room on Sept. 27, 1944 from what was ruled to have been an accidental overdose of sleeping pills.

One comment that was often heard from those paying their last respects to Aimee was, "There's the woman who led me to Jesus."[77] What better epitaph can any of us have?

Aimee Semple McPherson was a woman who believed that true revival comes when Christ is lifted up. Rev. William H.

Clagett, President of the Board of Trustees of Texas Presbyterian University in 1921 wrote of her, "I have never heard a preacher who seeks more sincerely to exalt Jesus Christ and who hides herself more completely behind Christ and His cross."[78]

Aimee wrote, "Through all the ages God has been seeking and using yielded and believing messengers through whom He could pour His message from Heaven to earth. The messenger must be in direct contact with the Lord and with the people, through a heart filled with love. God wants a Revival everywhere and is looking for empty vessels through which His message can flow. Such a messenger must not only take, believe and have confidence in the message, but must lose himself in it and be absorbed by it."[79]

This no doubt was the secret to Aimee's success. She was a yielded and believing messenger who challenges us today to become empty vessels whom God can use, filling us with love for His people and sending us out to bring His message of hope and healing to humanity.

Uldine Utley

"I praise Thee, O Father, Lord of heaven and earth, that Thou didst hide these things from the wise and intelligent and didst reveal them to babes. Yes, Father, for thus it was well-pleasing in Thy sight."
– Matthew 11: 25-26

"Blessed are the gentle, for they shall inherit the earth."
– Matthew 5: 5

Uldine Utley was radically saved at the age of nine. She had dreamed of becoming an actress and was about to get her first opportunity to perform in a play, but when she showed up for rehearsal, the door was locked. The location of the rehearsal had been changed, but her notification of that fact was lost in the mail. Her grandfather, who had taken her to the rehearsal, suggested she go with him instead to a revival meeting. Much peeved, she agreed to go, expecting to be bored to tears.

But the Holy Spirit spoke to her that day. She hung on every word the evangelist (Aimee Semple McPherson)[80] said, and when the invitation came, she made her way to the altar, weeping and praying, confessing her sins to God and receiving the cleansing forgiveness that He offered to her. Uldine went home that day a new creature in Christ.

Suddenly she had a burning desire to know more about God and His Word. She spent hours reading the Bible and praying. Her parents were saved at the same revival, so their home became filled with family devotions and Bible study. Shortly after that, Uldine prayed to receive the baptism of the Holy Spirit, which filled her heart with a love for the lost.

God had been so good to Uldine that it was natural for her to get up week after week in church and give a testimony. One day a missionary couple was visiting the church. After the service they asked Uldine to accompany them to the home of a large family and share her testimony there. She agreed to go, and after sharing in the family's meager repast, she gave her testimony. The father and three of the children received Christ that day.

The missionaries then asked her if she would accompany them to a neighboring town the next weekend and give her testimony again, this time at a revival meeting. With her parents' permission, she agreed to go. When they arrived, the church was packed. No sooner did she walk in the door, then she heard the pastor announce to the congregation that the "little evangelist" had arrived and he turned the entire service over to her! And so, at the age of ten, her preaching career was born. She was determined that none should know she was completely unprepared to lead the service, so she very calmly announced that they would begin by singing hymn number 157, not knowing at all what particular hymn that might be.

Years later, when recounting the incident, Uldine could not recall what she preached about that night, but she did remember that many men and women came to the altar to receive Christ's mercy for themselves. She was invited back to speak the next night as well, and then for several weekends after that.

Word got out about the little evangelist, and invitations began to come in from other towns. Uldine found she was traveling somewhere every weekend, preaching five to seven times from Friday night to Sunday. Eventually, invitations came from farther away and lasted longer than the weekend, so her parents had to hire a tutor for her. Her parents became her managers, planning the speaking events and handling the finances.

Before long they were crisscrossing the country. Uldine

spoke from California to New York and even into Canada, and down to Florida. She spoke at tent meetings and in churches, and also addressed a group of sailors aboard a naval ship. Sometimes her message was directed to those who did not yet know Christ, and other times to Christians who needed to come back to their first love.

In spite of her age, her sermons showed a careful understanding of language. She would often build her sermons around an analogy from everyday life, tying it to the truth of the Gospel. She backed up all her statements with scriptural references. Rather than preaching expository sermons, hers were more thematic, including bits of narrative in them. One reporter referred to her preaching style as "naïve and disarmingly forthright."[81]

Although Uldine Utley never achieved the prominence of D. L. Moody, Billy Sunday, or Billy Graham, hundreds of people confessed Christ as a result of her ministry. One magazine credited her with moving 10,000 men to change their behavior.[82] In addition to the preaching campaigns in various cities, she also published a magazine and spoke on the radio.

Journalists nicknamed her "Garbo of the Pulpit" and "Terror of the Tabernacles," but her mentor, Dr. John Roach Straton, a fundamentalist preacher from Calvary Baptist Church in New York, called her "Joan of Arc of the modern religious world."[83] At the age of 23 she was ordained "a deaconess with full right to the title Reverend" in the Methodist denomination.[84] Two years later, she married Wilbur Eugene Langkop.[85]

Uldine was often asked why she was a preacher. To many, it was inconceivable that a girl child should be a preacher. She replied:

> I am compelled to preach because of the love of Christ. He called me to preach, and I cannot fail to do what He asks. I delight too much in His will; I want His favor in

my life, too much. I put up no big profession; I agree with anybody who says it is foolish for a girl to preach. I honestly believe that, and I also believe what Paul says, 'It pleased God by the foolishness of preaching to save them that believe.' Listen, a moment. This Scripture says God saves men by the 'foolishness of preaching.' Then preaching is foolish, and if a girl preaching the Gospel is more foolish than a man preaching it, why should any objection be made, if souls can be saved through the method of preaching, which is more foolish?[86]

God's choices may not always be our choices, but He is the Sovereign, and I like to think He knows best. The important thing is for men and women, boys and girls to come to a saving knowledge of Jesus Christ. Why should anyone care how they get there?

Uldine's messages were easy to understand, but never condescending. She presented the Gospel in a manner that people could understand, but never compromised the truth. The simple Gospel of Jesus Christ, which she presented, drew people to the Cross.

Corrie ten Boom

I can do all things through Him who strengthens me.
– Philippians 4: 13

"Blessed are those who have been persecuted for the sake of righteousness, for theirs is the kingdom of heaven."
– Matthew 5: 10

Why would God choose Corrie ten Boom to tell the world of His love? To hear Corrie tell it, her sister Betsy was far more spiritual than she, yet Betsy died and Corrie became God's messenger. Betsy was one of those people who are so good, it's hard to believe they are real. In the concentration camp, Corrie saw a hell-hole; Betsy saw an opportunity to minister, not only to the other prisoners, but to the guards as well. Betsy could be thankful in all circumstances, even for biting fleas.

But in Corrie, we find a person that we can relate to. She shares her spiritual struggles and they are just like ours. Many prisoners, at first wondering what a gray-haired old lady could possibly say to them, found a person who was just like them, who could completely understand their situation because she had been there herself. Corrie ten Boom had walked a path few of us are ever called to walk, but through it she gained a testimony that would give others hope and point them in the way of the Savior. She is a spiritual giant, not because of a personality trait of her own, but because of what God was able to accomplish through her.

Corrie had the benefit of being raised in a family of Christians that went back for generations. Her great-grandfather, Gerrit ten Boom, was firm in his belief in the

Bible. He soundly rebuked his pastor one day for neglecting the Word of God. The pastor promised to do better the following Sunday, to which Gerrit replied, "If God grants you the time to do so."[87] The pastor died before Sunday came.

Gerrit's son Willem, Corrie's grandfather, was also an outspoken critic of the liberal theology being taught throughout Europe in those days. He also stood out for his love for the Jews. In 1844, one hundred years before Corrie and her family were arrested for hiding Jews from the Nazis, Willem started a weekly prayer meeting for Israel. He passed this love for the Jews on to his children and grandchildren. Corrie's brother Willem recognized the racism behind the rising hatred for Jews and wrote a doctoral thesis entitled "The Birth of Modern Racial Anti-Semitism in France and Germany," which was published in 1928.

Corrie arrived in the world prematurely. She was the youngest of four children and was so pitifully small at birth that she was not expected to live. But God had a plan for her and so she grew into a healthy young girl.

Corrie was bothered by nightmares as a small child, but at her mother's request, she invited Jesus into her heart when she was only five years old, and that was the end of her troubled nights. Corrie was a bit of a tomboy as a child and was not as pretty as her sisters. Yet she grew up in a household filled with the love of Christ. In addition to her mother, father, and three siblings, three aunts, sisters of Mama, all lived with the ten Booms in their odd shaped house, called the Beje.

Mama and the aunts suffered from ill health. Tante Bep died from tuberculosis, and then Tante Jans was diagnosed with diabetes. Corrie was trained to test Tante Jans' blood sugar weekly. If the test turned black, death would be imminent. On the day the test turned black, Corrie went to her father. She assured him she had performed the test correctly and so the family went together to deliver the news to Tante Jans, who died a few days later.

Tante Jans had been very active in spreading the gospel. She had organized services for soldiers and allowed Corrie to participate by singing and sharing her testimony.

When Corrie was a teenager, she was misdiagnosed with tuberculosis and sent to bed for five months. She grumbled about her fate but spent the time reading her bible and studying church history. She also found herself spending more and more time in prayer. When her illness turned out to be appendicitis, she was easily treated and cured, but the time had been valuable for her. In addition to drawing closer to God, she had also made some concrete plans for her future. She would go to college.

Upon receiving her teaching credentials, Corrie got a job as a governess and moved in with a wealthy family. Corrie was not happy in that situation, because the people were not Christians. The father had even made an improper sexual advance toward Corrie. So when her brother Willem showed up one day to say her help was needed at home, Corrie was glad to go.

Corrie helped around the house while her oldest sister Betsy worked in the watch shop helping Papa. Through an illness of Betsy's it was discovered that they were both in the wrong place. Corrie had a head for business and was much happier working in the watch shop, while Betsy preferred the domestic duties. Each excelled in their new tasks.

Eventually, Corrie went to school in Switzerland to learn watch making. She became the first female watchmaker in Holland.[88]

Neither Betsy nor Corrie ever married. Betsy suffered from pernicious anemia and so she chose to remain single. Corrie had fallen in love with a young man who broke her heart, and she never loved another.

She had met Karel through her brother. They were friends in college, both of them studying to be pastors. At Willem's wedding, Corrie and Karel became reacquainted. They saw each other again when Willem preached his first sermon. They took walks together and began to talk about the future. Willem soon burst Corrie's bubble, though, by telling her that Karel's parents expected him to marry a woman of means, and he would not disappoint them. True to Willem's prediction, one day Karel showed up at the Beje with a woman on his arm, whom he introduced to Corrie as his fiancee. Corrie's father encouraged her to give her broken heart to the Lord, and let God redirect her love where it would be welcomed.

World War I came and went, with Holland remaining neutral. Shortly after the war ended, Corrie's mother suffered a stroke, which left her able to speak only three words, "yes," "no," and "Corrie." Communication was difficult but not impossible. Two years later, Mama's speech had not improved. Corrie's next older sister Nollie was to be married, and Mama was sad that she could not have a mother-daughter premarital talk with Nollie. On the day of the wedding, the final hymn was Mama's favorite, "Fairest Lord Jesus." To everyone's amazement, Mama sang the entire hymn. Afterward, she could again speak only her three words. One month later she died.

The ten Booms, used to having lots of people in their home, began taking in foster children. They started taking in the children of missionaries, as a way of contributing to the work of missions. In addition to the foster children, Corrie began working with retarded children. She discovered that they were eager to learn about Jesus and experienced God in remarkable ways.

Corrie also started a girls' club, which grew and grew, as the need was great. The clubs grew so rapidly, they became the foundation for Girl Guides in Holland. Later, though, when it seemed to Corrie that the Girl Guides were abandoning their Christian standards, substituting moral instruction, she pulled away and started Netherlands Girls' Clubs, dedicated to

Christian principles.[89] There is no telling how many young lives the ten Booms touched during the years between the world wars.

Yet war was once again on the horizon. Papa, Betsy, and Corrie, now alone in the Beje, could hear the ranting of a madman over the radio, as Germany began to threaten their neighbors. Even Holland, who had declared its neutrality, was not spared. Germany invaded and Holland fell on May 10, 1940.

As an occupied nation, the Dutch were ordered to turn in their radios (the newspapers were already under the control of the Germans). The ten Boom household contained two radios, but they only turned in one, so they could keep abreast of news coming from somewhere other than Germany. Corrie, who turned their radio in, was shocked to discover how easy it was to lie when asked if there were other radios in their household.

Shortly after that Corrie was unable to sleep one night because of the fighting planes overhead. She heard Betsy in the kitchen, so she went down for a cup of tea. When she returned to her room, she found a large piece of shrapnel on her pillow. She and Betsy thanked God for His hand of protection.

One night Corrie had a vision. She saw four black horses pulling a wagon through Harlem, where they lived. In the wagon was her whole family – Papa, Betsy, Corrie, Willem, Nollie, and her nephew Peter. Corrie wondered what it meant.

She began to see Jews being singled out for mistreatment. Jews were disappearing. No one knew where. The ten Booms' neighbor, Mr. Weil, was thrust out of his fur shop. His wife was not at home. Corrie knew Mrs. Weil must be warned not to come home, but she didn't know how to reach her. She decided to turn to her brother Willem. He would know what to do. Later that evening, Corrie's nephew Kik arrived to take Mr. Weil away. When Corrie asked after him two weeks later, Kik admonished her for asking questions about underground proceedings. Corrie struggled to understand her new role as a Christian engaged in illegal activities.

As more and more Jews were being arrested, Corrie prayed, "Lord Jesus, I offer myself for Your people. In any way. Any place. Any time."[90] As she prayed, she again had the vision of four black horses leading her family away in a wagon.

One or two at a time, Jews began showing up at the Beje, with what few belongings they could carry. Ration cards had to be stolen for them, and then they were moved to safer spots. Corrie realized more than ever that she would have to rely on God's guidance. He alone knew who could be trusted and who could not.

As the danger mounted, they constructed a secret room in Corrie's bedroom where the Jews could hide. They installed alarms and practiced getting into the hiding place and removing all evidence of extra residents.

On February 28, 1944, the house was raided. Corrie was sick with the flu and a weekly prayer meeting led by Willem was going on in the house. Corrie heard the alarm, but at first was too ill to react, until she saw their houseguests clearly frightened and disappearing into the hiding place. One woman was wheezing with asthma. Corrie prayed, asking Jesus to heal her so she would not give everyone away.

When a German soldier burst into her room and ordered her to get up and get dressed, she hurried to obey, in order to get the man out of the room as quickly as possible. Yet, she heard not a sound from the secret room.

Downstairs, Corrie was taken aside and interrogated. As the blows rained down on her face she cried out to Jesus for protection. Her attacker then threatened to kill her if she so much as mentioned that name again, as if the very Name itself had power to undo him, as of course it does. Then he led her back to the dining room and tried in vain to get information from Betsy.

Corrie and her entire family were taken into custody. They spent the night at the police station and the next day were taken to prison. As the bus hauled them away, Corrie remembered her vision. It had come true.

Because of his advanced age of 84, Corrie's father was given the opportunity to be sent home, provided he promised to behave himself. Papa replied that his door would always be open to those in need. The officer angrily withdrew his offer and Papa was sent to prison, where he died nine days later.

All the rest of the family were eventually released, except Corrie and Betsy, as well as their nephew Kik, who was later sent to a concentration camp where he died. Nollie sent packages to her incarcerated sisters. Because of her illness, Corrie was placed in a cell by herself. She had several opportunities to talk with a lieutenant, sharing Jesus with him. Whether he ever opened his heart to the Lord, Corrie never learned.

Late in the month of June, the prison was hurriedly evacuated. The prisoners assumed the allies were approaching. They were moved to a concentration camp called Vught. Betsy was assigned to a sewing detail, while Corrie went to work in a radio factory. Because of her experience as a watchmaker, she was put to work assembling the intricate radio wiring. The radios were put in German fighter planes, so the workers, including Corrie, purposely made them defective.

While in Vught, they learned the name of the man who betrayed them, Jan Vogel. Corrie was filled with such violent hatred for the man that she made herself physically ill. When she asked Betsy why she wasn't just as angry with him, Betsy replied that she felt terribly sorry for him and prayed for him every time his name came to her mind. Knowing that she had committed murder in her heart, Corrie turned to Jesus and forgave Jan Vogel, and asked for forgiveness for her own wicked thoughts. Peace returned to her once again.

When next the allies got too close, the prisoners were packed into a freight train and transported over four days into Germany. Their final destination this time was Ravensbruck.

Their first two nights at Ravensbruck were spent sleeping on the ground outside, even in the rain. When finally they were processed into the camp, Corrie saw that they would be required to strip naked, walk past several male guards into the shower room, and come back out wearing only a thin prison dress and shoes. It would be impossible to smuggle precious belongings past the guards. Corrie and Betsy had a sweater that Betsy needed, as well as a bottle of vitamin oil and their Bible. As their turn to strip drew closer, Corrie began to pray. Immediately Betsy became sick. Corrie asked a guard if they could use the restroom. He directed them to the shower room. No one was in there at the time and Corrie spotted a place where they could hide their precious contraband. When they returned later for their showers, Corrie tucked the belongings under her dress, trying as best she could to hide its bulk. When they came out, all the women were being frisked, but for some reason no one touched her. Yet another search was going on further down the line. Corrie slowed up, expecting to be searched, but she was roughly shoved and told to move along.

The Bible, vitamins, and sweater made it into Ravensbruck with them, the first of many miracles they would experience in that concentration camp. Corrie and Betsy celebrated the amazing power of God. In spite of the hell all around them, Corrie and Betsy were able to brighten the spirits of the women around them by sharing God's love and Word.

Miracles continued to come in odd ways. Betsy's bottle of vitamin oil never ran dry, even though she was sharing it with many other women. Corrie couldn't believe it could still produce drops for such a long time, but it did. Then one day another prisoner gave them some vitamins she had managed to smuggle out of the hospital. That night Betsy's bottle was dry.

Betsy and Corrie were assigned to a barracks that was infested with fleas. Betsy reminded Corrie that they were to give thanks in all circumstances, and so she gave thanks for the fleas. Corrie was sure she had flipped this time.

Every chance they got, they led a Bible study to an ever-increasing number of women. Corrie couldn't understand why the guards, so maddeningly present throughout the camp, left their barracks totally unsupervised. They were free to share the gospel of Jesus Christ to all who would listen in their barracks. One day Corrie discovered the reason the guards avoided their barracks – the fleas. From then on even she could give thanks for the fleas.

Their labor in the camp was grueling and their food barely enough to keep them alive. Betsy grew weaker and weaker and was finally sick enough to be admitted to the hospital. A few days later she was returned to her barracks, but reassigned to the knitting brigade. Some time later Corrie was also assigned with the knitters. Without interference from the guards, they used the time to minister to their fellow inmates. Their barracks became a center for prayer in the camp.

One night Corrie heard that 250 younger, stronger Dutch people were being moved to another factory. Corrie risked her life to climb out a window and whisper encouragement to them as they passed. They all survived, save one.[91]

Betsy and Corrie began to talk about what they would do after the war. They would run a shelter in Holland for survivors of concentration camps. Betsy described the house they would have as though she saw it perfectly. Shortly before Christmas Betsy was again so ill she needed to go to the hospital. Before she left she told Corrie they must also run a camp in Germany, where those who had been taught to hate could learn to love again. She prophesied that she and Corrie would both be freed before the new year.

Betsy's freedom came a few days later in the hospital. Corrie sneaked to the hospital and looked in the window where Betsy lay. At first she didn't realized that the yellowed, skeletal figure she was seeing was her sister, but then the truth sunk in. Betsy's body was taken away to a bathroom that served as a morgue. Corrie wanted to look again, but couldn't bring herself to do so. Then a friend who worked in the hospital caught her arm and took her to where Betsy's body lay. Another miracle had happened. Betsy's emaciated form had been restored to it's pre-prison appearance. She appeared to be sleeping, healthy, and, to Corrie, altogether lovely, a foretaste of the glorious resurrection to come.

Three days after Betsy's death, Corrie's name was called at roll call. Her release had come. Though she had to spend a few more agonizing days in the hospital before she was allowed to leave, she eventually found herself on a train headed out of Germany. New Year 1945 had come. Corrie later learned that her release had been a mistake. One week after she was set free, women her age were executed.

Returning to Holland, Corrie found herself in a hospital where she was treated with such kindness and consideration, she hardly knew how to react. She had become so used to brutality and inhumanity that kindness totally took her by surprise. She sobbed with joy, recognizing that the rest of her life was a gift from God. She wrote, "I knew my life had been given back for a purpose. I was no longer my own. This time I had been ransomed and released. I knew that God would soon be sending me out as a tramp for the Lord. But right now, He was letting me enjoy the luxury of thanksgiving. I was drinking from a fountain I knew would never run dry – the fountain of praise."[92]

Returning to her home was a difficult task, since Holland was still occupied and war damage was everywhere, but eventually she was back home, repairing watches once again.

Yet there was a restlessness in her soul. She remembered

Betsy's words, that they must tell others what they had learned from their ordeal, and so she began to speak. After one such talk, a lady came up and offered her home in gratitude for God's protection of her sons, working in the underground. The mansion fit Betsy's description perfectly. In May of that year Holland was freed from German occupation and the first residents in the mansion began to arrive. Many of them were people who had been in hiding throughout the war.

Corrie opened up the Beje to the most despised Hollanders – those who had sided with Germany during the war, betraying their own countrymen. They were the ones the Dutch found hardest to forgive, but with forgiveness came healing and vice versa.

Forgiveness became a prominent theme for Corrie in her ministry. She who had been so wronged by her fellow human beings knew the healing that can only come from forgiveness. In her work after the war with those whose lives had been torn apart by the war, she saw that those who were able to forgive were able to return to a semi-normal life much sooner than those who would not forgive. Those who would not forgive carried a load of anger and bitterness that precluded their healing.

Corrie's understanding of the power of forgiveness had not come easily. She often preached on the necessity of forgiveness, citing *Matthew 6: 14-15*, which reads, "For if you forgive men for their transgressions, your heavenly Father will also forgive you. But if you do not forgive men, then your Father will not forgive your transgressions." After one such sermon one of her former captors at Ravensbruck came forward. She knew him at once and her blood ran cold. The man explained that he had become a Christian after the war. God had forgiven him, but he wanted Corrie's forgiveness as well, and he held out his hand to her.

Corrie had no power in herself to take the man's hand and

forgive him, yet she knew she must do it. Having no other recourse but the love of Christ, she silently prayed. She could supply the mechanics, if Jesus would supply the love and forgiveness. She forced herself to take the man's hand, and when she did so, the love of Christ flowed through her and she was truly able to forgive him with her whole heart.[93]

After the war, the man who had betrayed the ten Booms was convicted as a war criminal and executed. Corrie, who had learned to forgive, corresponded with him and led him to the Lord before he died.

Corrie traveled the world with her message of God's love. Getting to America after the war was difficult because of travel and immigration restrictions, but the Lord made a way for her and provided places for her to stay and speak. Then she returned to Europe and even to Germany. A former concentration camp at Darmstadt was turned into a refuge for homeless Germans, as another of Betsy's visions came true.

For the next ten years, Corrie continued traveling and speaking. One day she found herself in Switzerland and couldn't remember why she was there or whom she was supposed to meet. She decided to return to Holland, which she did, but before she could get to where she was going, she fell and injured her hip. The doctor said she must rest for several weeks for it to heal. That would never do. She needed to be in Germany for a student conference in a few days. In frustration over her slow recovery, she cried out, "Is there not a Christian in all Harlem who can pray for me to be healed?"[94] A minister was called in. Corrie confessed her sin and the man laid hands on her and prayed. She got more than she bargained for. Instead of just healing of her body, she found herself immersed in the love of Christ, with joy unspeakable, as she received the baptism of the Holy Spirit. She was 63 years old and had served the Lord all of her life, but from that point on she found a new power for ministry.

After twelve years of traveling alone, Corrie acquired a companion named Connie. When Connie married, another Dutch woman, named Ellen, became Corrie's traveling companion.

Corrie once spoke at a girl's school in Washington, DC. One woman remarked, "The atmosphere of the hall was electric with spiritual power."[95] The girls were expecting yet another boring missionary, but recognized the voice of the Lord speaking through Corrie.

Sometimes Corrie had to battle demons. In a trip behind the Iron Curtain, she preached her heart out, but the people sat like stones. She sensed that they wanted to respond to her message but were unable to break free from the bondage that held them. On the last night of the meetings, Corrie interrupted her message and commanded the demons to leave in the Name of Jesus. The whole atmosphere changed and the people were able to receive Christ. Afterwards, the local pastors were worried because such a thing was forbidden in communist countries. Corrie's simple response was, "I had to obey God."[96]

Corrie's holocaust experience allowed her to reach people who were also imprisoned. She often visited prisons, many with conditions as miserable as Ravensbruck. At first the prisoners would stare at her, wondering what this old woman could possibly know of their lot. Then she would share a story of Ravensbruck, its misery and the victory she gained through Christ's presence with her, and the prisoners would know that she was one of them. God sustained her through her prison experience and He could sustain them as well. The response to her ministry was dramatic.

In a country in Africa Christians were being martyred. Corrie held a service and addressed the fear she saw on the people's faces. She preached from *1 Peter 4: 12-14*, a passage on suffering for the Lord, and shared with them a piece of wisdom she had received from her father when she was a young child. As a child she had been afraid that she would not have the strength to be a martyr for Christ. Her father pointed out to her that when they took a train ride, he held on to her ticket until just before it was time to board. He assured her that our Heavenly Father is just as careful about giving to us what we need at the time that we need it. The people found renewed strength that night, and that week many of them were martyred.

One time, crossing into Russia with a suitcase full of Bibles, Corrie prayed as she saw the customs officers checking everyone's bags. When she opened her eyes, she got a glimpse of the light of angels surrounding her suitcase. She passed through customs with no trouble.

After twenty years of traveling the world, Corrie was granted a year off. Her health demanded the rest. When the year ended it was difficult for Corrie to get excited about resuming her travels. Retirement looked so attractive, but God was not finished with her yet. He had many more people for Corrie to touch, so she repented of her "laziness" and kept going, even though she was well into her seventies.

In August of 1978, she suffered a debilitating stroke and was bedridden for the rest of her life. Like her mother so many years before, communication became very difficult. Corrie was now on the receiving end of love and caring. On her 91st birthday, April 15, 1983, she slipped away to join her family and be at last, eternally with the Lord she had served so faithfully.

Corrie ten Boom was a woman with an abiding faith in God. Jamie Buckingham wrote of her: "As a little girl believes her Daddy can do anything, so Corrie ten Boom trusts in God – even more."[97]

She was not perfect, but she sought always to grow in Christ and become more obedient to His will. Carole Carlson wrote, "Corrie never felt that she had 'arrived' in her spiritual knowledge. She was always learning, always seeking to know more of God's will for her."[98]

Corrie was an ordinary person, but one whose love for the Lord and love for her fellow human beings led her to give her life to the furtherance of the Gospel. Her message was simple and her testimony was compelling. She knew the truth behind the words she spoke, and would not compromise that truth. She carried the message of God's love around the world, touching souls only God can count. Through her books, her story of triumph in the face of all the devil can throw at a person continues to touch people everywhere.

Kathryn Kuhlman

"And these signs will accompany those who have believed: in My name they will cast out demons, they will speak with new tongues; they will pick up serpents, and if they drink any deadly poison, it shall not hurt them; they will lay hands on the sick, and they will recover."
– Mark 16: 17-18

"Blessed are the merciful, for they shall receive mercy."
– Matthew 5: 7

Kathryn Kuhlman was a woman fully surrendered to God, and because of her total surrender, God used her in powerful ways. She was an imperfect vessel, and she knew better than anyone that, without the Holy Spirit, she could do nothing. But with Him, anything was possible.

Kathryn was born in Concordia, Missouri on May 9, 1907.[99] The date was recorded in the family bible, otherwise we would not have known it, since Kathryn was never truthful about her age. Her parents were Joseph Kuhlman and Emma Walkenhorst. Emma was a devout Methodist, while Joe was a nominal Baptist. He disliked preachers and would cross the street to avoid them.

Kathryn adored her father. Her mother was the stricter disciplinarian, and Kathryn seemed to be always striving for her approval. No doubt she exasperated her mother, for she was a mischievous child.

At school she was the class clown and a great story teller. She had a flair for the dramatic, even at an early age, and seemed to enjoy being the center of attention. She said she had a slight stutter as a child, so her mother encouraged her to speak very slowly and enunciate her words very carefully. As an adult she was often criticized for the way she talked and for her dramatic style, but according to her elder sister Myrtle, she had always been that way.

Kathryn attended church and Sunday school regularly with her mother, who was a beloved teacher of youth at the church. One day, when Kathryn was fourteen, the words of the pastor pierced her heart during the worship service and she recognized her sinfulness and her need of a Savior. She moved to the front pew and wept. Later, when she returned home, she told her father that Jesus had come into her heart that day.

Kathryn's older sister Myrtle had married an evangelist, Everett Parrott, and the two of them were traveling the country holding tent meetings. The summer after her sophomore year in high school, Kathryn went with them. It was her first taste of life as an itinerant minister. Although Everett never allowed her to preach, he did ask her on several occasions to share her testimony.

The following autumn, rather than returning to Missouri, Kathryn enrolled in Simpson Bible Institute in Seattle. Kathryn never spoke of this time in her life. Although she was a good student, she was not always a good girl, and it is possible she was expelled for misbehavior.[100]

From there she went to Los Angeles, possibly attending Aimee Semple McPherson's L.I.F.E. Bible School,[101] though that cannot be verified. Aimee's own set of scandals could have been the reason Kathryn kept silent about having sat temporarily at her feet.

So Kathryn set out once again with Myrtle and Everett. Their marriage was rocky and they would often get into spats. After one such spat, Everett left, taking the money with him. Myrtle, Kathryn, and their musician Helen Gulliford were alone. Myrtle decided to go to her husband, but Kathryn and

Helen chose to set out on their own, visiting little churches in Idado and Montana.

They traveled throughout Idaho, preaching in every little town they came to. Although they had a very small beginning, by the time they reached Twin Falls, Kathryn preached to over two thousand people, with 218 responding to the altar calls.

After five years in Idaho, they traveled to Colorado, eventually holding meetings in a warehouse in Denver. Kathryn had no desire to put down roots and pastor a church. She believed men made better pastors. She preferred to think of herself as an evangelist. However, the people of Denver did not want her to leave, so they gathered their money and bought a building, which was renovated into a nondenominational tabernacle where Kathryn served as their minister.

Sadly, Kathryn's father never heard her preach. He died after an accident while she was in Denver, Dec. 30, 1934. It was the most painful experience of her life up to that point. She drove through ice and snow to return to Missouri, but her heart was full of anger and bitterness. She could not bring herself to look at him in the coffin. Finally, at the end of the funeral service, she was the last one to go by the coffin before it was closed forever. She reached out to touch the shoulder where she had often laid her head, and realized that it was not her father who lay there. Her father was gone and it was only an empty vessel in the coffin. Kathryn considered that experience her first healing, because the anger and bitterness were gone.[102]

Returning to Denver, Kathryn's life was about to take another very unpleasant turn. She would learn very painfully what it means to be totally surrendered to God.

Kathryn often invited other evangelists to speak at her tabernacle in Denver. One of these evangelists was Burroughs A. Waltrip, a handsome but very married man. Kathryn fell head-over-heels in love with him. In 1937 he divorced his wife, leaving her to raise their two children on her own. Somehow he was able to convince Kathryn that his wife had left him. She believed it because she very much wanted to believe it, and thus justify her own marriage to him.

Waltrip had gone to Mason City, Iowa, and, despite financial hard times brought about by the Depression, was able to raise enough money and procure enough loans to build an elaborate church. Kathryn was a frequent guest speaker, but in the fall of 1938 the church was already falling into financial trouble. In October he and Kathryn were married.

Kathryn's Denver congregation was stunned. His previous marriage disqualified him as a suitable husband for their pastor. Kathryn's closest friends and advisors had begged her not to do it, but she would listen to no one.

According to friends, Kathryn realized as soon as the wedding ceremony was over that she had made a mistake and was out of God's will. She would not enter the hotel with Waltrip on their wedding night, but left him, determined to seek an annulment. She and her friends drove back to Denver. Kathryn intended to apologize to her congregation and seek their forgiveness, only to find that they had shut her out. Dejected, she returned to her husband.[103]

The tabernacle congregation in Denver fell apart. The building was sold to an Assemblies of God church, but was never the same. Similarly, financial troubles beset the elaborate church in Mason City, until the doors were closed in May of 1939.

The Waltrips went on the road to evangelize, working several cities, sometimes together, sometimes apart. Kathryn loved her husband, yet in the eyes of God, it seemed their relationship was adulterous, since he had deserted his lawful wife.

Kathryn went through an agonizing period of wrestling with God, wanting His blessing back, no matter what it took. She described a Saturday afternoon when she fully surrendered to the Holy Spirit. She said, "Then I knew what the scripture meant about taking up your cross. A cross is the symbol of death. That afternoon, Kathryn Kuhlman died. And when I died, God came in, the Holy Spirit came in. There, for the first time, I realized what it meant to have power."[104] Kathryn left Waltrip and probably never saw him again. Some time later he sued for divorce.

She went to Franklin, Pennsylvania for a two-week visit, but ending up staying for several years. The people there loved her and accepted her, in spite of her now shaded past. And she loved them. While in Franklin, she began preaching on the radio. Tapes were kept of her broadcasts and were even played for several years after her death.

In Franklin, she again began small. Her first night, there were only 38 people in attendance, but the second night there were nearly 200. After that, the services were packed to overflowing every night.

Because of her own recent, powerful experience with the Holy Spirit, she began preaching about Him and the resurrection power. On the third night that she was in Franklin she started again to preach about the Holy Spirit when a woman came forward and interrupted her, asking to share her testimony. The woman told how she had been in the audience the night before. As Kathryn preached about the power of the Holy Spirit, the woman felt the power of God going through her, and she knew she was healed. The next day she went to her doctor, who confirmed that her tumor was gone.[105] It was Kathryn's first public miracle, and had happened spontaneously, without her knowledge. Just as in *Acts 10: 44*, where the Holy Spirit fell upon those who were listening to Peter preach, so also the Holy Spirit fell on this woman when Kathryn Kuhlman preached.

From that time on, the miracles kept coming. George Orr had been injured in an industrial accident years before when liquid iron splashed upon his eyelid and burned through to the eye, leaving a scar on his cornea. The scar tissue completely blocked the vision in that eye. By 1947, his other eye was showing signs of strain from having to do all the work. On May 4th of that year he attended Kathryn's service. When she preached that healing was possible, he prayed for healing and the scar tissue was removed. He returned to his doctor, who was stunned.[106]

Mary Schmidt was healed of a goiter. Another person, Millie Heldman, was seated behind her and watched the goiter disappear. Millie had come to the meeting a skeptic, but that night she went to the altar and gave her life to the Lord. She served with Kathryn for thirty years.

Kathryn moved on to Pittsburgh, filling Carnegie Hall. But she hesitated to move there permanently, not wanting to leave the good people of Franklin. She told her assistant Maggie that the roof of her Faith Temple in Franklin would have to cave in to convince her God wanted her to move on. On Thanksgiving Day in 1950 it did precisely that – too much snow caused the roof to collapse.[107]

Kathryn preached in Carnegie Hall until it was closed for renovations in 1967. Then she moved to the First Presbyterian Church at the invitation of the pastor, Dr. Robert Lamont and his board of elders. She regularly held miracle services on Friday mornings. Kathryn stayed in Pittsburgh for the rest of her life. She was reluctant to move from there, but after receiving many invitations to preach elsewhere, she finally agreed to go on the road. In 1965 she went to California, eventually preaching in Aimee Semple McPherson's Angelus Temple. She also preached in such places as Boston, Providence, R.I., Las Vegas, and into Canada.

Many, many people were healed in her services, but far more went away without the physical healing that they were seeking. Early in her career, Kathryn had visited a meeting conducted by a faith healer. There she saw that those who were not healed were told that it was their own lack of faith that kept them from being healed. Thus in addition to their physical ailment, they also went home with a new load of guilt. Kathryn wept when she saw it.

Her own theology of healing had changed throughout the years. Early on, she too had believed that if one had the right amount of faith and did everything that was required, healing would come. But in her services she saw that many of the people who were healed had little or no faith at all. Even self-proclaimed atheists were healed. At the same time, some very godly believers went away without physical healing. Kathryn came to realize that healing is a sovereign act of God. He alone makes the decision as to who will be healed and who will not.

Of far more importance than physical healing was the state of one's spiritual health. Kathryn Kuhlman tried to keep the emphasis on salvation, saying, "Don't come forward unless you are willing to give your heart to Jesus Christ."[108]

Still, Kathryn's heart broke for those who were not healed. She once related an incident in which she met with a reporter from the Kansas City *Star* after a miracle service. She told the reporter that she was grateful for those who were healed, but wept for those who were not. A few days later she got a letter from the reporter. The reporter wrote that she had attended the miracle service with a friend who was in the last stages of terminal cancer. Her friend was not healed, but died within a week after the service. Even so, the ailing man said attending the service was the best thing that had ever happened to him. Although he was not healed physically, he had surrendered his life to Christ. His final days were marked with the peace that comes from knowing one's sins are forgiven and his final destination secured.

Of course, there were many skeptics. Some claimed that all the cured illnesses were psychosomatic. Others claimed that

Kathryn Kuhlman hypnotized people, or that their supposed healing was only a temporary remission. Allen Spraggett, who investigated several of the healings, concluded that they were genuine, but gave the credit to parapsychology, not God.[109]

Kathryn herself set strict standards for any miracles that were reported in any of her books or shared on her television show. Jamie Buckingham wrote:

> 1. The disease or injury should be organic or structural in nature – and should have been medically diagnosed.
> 2. The healing should have occurred rapidly, or instantaneously. The changes would have to be abnormal, and not the kind that would result from suggestion.
> 3. All healings would have to be medically verified – preferably by more than one doctor. At least one of the doctors must be the patient's private physician.
> 4. The healing should be permanent, or at least of sufficient duration so as not to be diagnosed as a 'remission'.[110]

One skeptic, Dr. William A. Nolen, wrote a scathing attack after attending one of Kathryn's miracle services. He investigated many of the people who thought they had been healed and could not find one who actually had been, so he denounced her entire ministry. In many cases, the people had never had their illnesses diagnosed in the first place. In response, another doctor, H. Richard Casdorph, investigated several other claimed healings and concluded that they were genuine.[111]

The stories of healings continued to pour in throughout Kathryn's career. Captain John LeVrier was told by three doctors that he would die. Cancer had spread to the blood and bone marrow. After he attended a miracle service, he returned to his doctors. Dr. Lowell S. Miller of M. D. Anderson Hospital and Tumor Institute in Houston said, "I could not find a single trace of cancer after he visited [the miracle service in] California. And with the type of cancer he had, there is no spontaneous remission." Dr. Ardean J. Ediger of Boise, Idaho, also documented LeVrier's cure. He had considered LeVrier's cancer incurable.[112] LeVrier, who had come to the service a nominal Christian, went on to have a healing ministry of his own, giving the glory to God.

At a healing service in Las Vegas in 1975, 12-year-old Douglas Hall was cured of rheumatoid arthritis. He hadn't grown at all in six years and went to Kathryn's service in a wheelchair. He walked onto the stage, saying he was healed. His parents later said the boy grew five inches and gained nine pounds in the ensuing months. He still needed surgery to remove calcium deposits from his hip sockets, but he continued to make good progress.[113]

Marjorie Close had been diagnosed with stomach cancer and given six weeks to live. She reluctantly went to Kathryn's meeting in Pittsburgh and was healed. She went to the altar where she confessed she did not know Jesus. Kathryn led her in the sinner's prayer and she went home to lead her family to the Lord. The one person who refused to believe in Marjorie's healing was her pastor. He attributed Kathryn Kuhlman's power to the devil.[114]

One Canadian woman, Mary Pettigrew, traveled to Pittsburgh for a healing service. Mary suffered from multiple sclerosis. She had to use braces and a walker to walk, and suffered from spasms. At the meeting, she felt a spasm coming on and had to be helped out of the auditorium. In the lobby, she passed out. When she came to, her husband helped her up and she discovered she was able to walk normally. The MS was gone and would never come back.[115]

Mary took it upon herself to organize bus trips to Kathryn's services, so others could find hope in Christ. When Kathryn spread her ministry to Canada, Mary Pettigrew became a very capable leader there.

Kathryn also had the opportunity to minister to her own mother. Her mother Emma had not totally approved of Kathryn's vocation, but after the death of Kathryn's father, Emma went to hear Kathryn preach. She preached on the Holy Spirit and invited those who wanted salvation or a deeper walk with the Holy Spirit to go into a back room. As she was praying for people, in walked Emma. At first Kathryn thought her mother was just there as a spectator, but Emma informed her that she was responding to the invitation. She wanted to know Jesus more. Emma went to her knees and Kathryn laid hands on her and prayed. Emma began to weep, then lifted up her voice and praised God in an unknown language. Then she told Kathryn never to stop preaching, "that others might receive what I have just received."[116]

Kathryn was completely in control of her meetings. In an effort to keep the meetings ecumenical, she would not allow speaking in tongues, so as not to alienate those for whom that practice was suspect. She would also silence those who felt called upon to stand and give a prophecy. For this she received much criticism from her Pentecostal brothers and sisters, but she insisted on keeping her meetings orderly and free from fanaticism. Even so, they were highly emotional services. Jamie Buckingham believed that part of the reason the power of God was so evident in her meetings was because she kept everything focused and concentrated on God.[117]

A common phenomenon in her meetings was the vast number of people "falling under the power," or being "slain in the Spirit." The presence of God so filled the room that people were unable to remain on their feet.

Kathryn wrote, "Many are the times when the Power of the Holy Ghost is so present in my own body that I have to struggle to remain on my feet. Many are the times when His Very Presence healed sick bodies before my eyes; my mind is so surrendered to the Spirit, that I know the exact body being healed: the sickness, the affliction, and in some instances, the very sin in their lives."[118]

Oral Roberts said of her, "The Holy Spirit was as real to her, more real, than any person around her. They were so wrapped up in each other – she and the Holy Spirit – that they talked back and forth and you never could tell when the Holy Spirit started and Kathryn left off. They were one."[119]

Clearly the healings came from the power of the Holy Spirit and not from anything Kathryn Kuhlman did. Jamie Buckingham observed that Kathryn received thousands of letters from people requesting prayer, but that there was no evidence that she ever prayed for the specific requests.[120] Even so, many people had their requests granted. For example, *Time* magazine reported that Mrs. Myrtle Joseph of Youngstown, OH, who suffered from lymphatic leukemia, wrote a letter to Kathryn asking for her prayers. A few days later she was healed.[121]

Kathryn's fame was worldwide. In 1972 she had an audience with Pope Paul, who said to her, "You're doing an admirable job. You not only have my blessing, you have my prayers."[122]

The Kathryn Kuhlman Foundation was a strong supporter of foreign missions. They provided the funding for building churches in many other countries, turning them over to the native people when they were built. Kathryn also visited South Viet Nam during the war and funded the building of a military chapel. She also gave wheelchairs for paraplegics and was given a medal of honor from the government of South Viet Nam.[123]

Kathryn also spoke at the World Conference on the Holy Spirit in Israel in 1975, ministering in Jerusalem and Tel Aviv.

Back home, though, life was not all roses for Kathryn

Kuhlman. She was criticized because she enjoyed the fine things of life that success can bring, such as expensive clothes. She also enjoyed antiques and fine art and was an avid collector. Many of these items were gifts given by grateful people to whom Kathryn had ministered.[124]

There were also rumors of scandals among her staff. The worst such scandal surrounded two former employees, Dino Kartsonakis, a pianist, and his brother-in-law, Paul Bartholomew. They sued her, and threatened to print a nasty book about her. The case was settled out of court, costing Kathryn plenty.[125]

Kathryn Kuhlman, a conduit of healing for so many others, was denied healing for her own heart ailment. She who seemed to have inexhaustible energy, failed to heed her doctor's advice that she slow down, until she finally collapsed and was hospitalized late in 1975. She died on Feb. 20, 1976.

Kathryn had said, "If after I am gone just one person can stand by my grave and say, 'I found Christ because she preached the Gospel,' then I will not have lived in vain."[126] Many people found Christ as a result of Kathryn Kuhlman's preaching. Many of those have gone on to have ministries of their own, broadening her influence.

Ruth Atkins, a friend from Kathryn's Franklin, PA, days, said, "Kathryn Kuhlman more than any one person has made Jesus real to me."[127] Kathryn Kuhlman did not live in vain.

End Notes

1. Helen Kooiman Hosier, *Kathryn Kuhlman* (Old Tappan, NJ: Fleming H. Revell Company, 1976), 99.

2. Regine Pernoud, *Joan of Arc*, translated by Edward Hyams (New York: Stein and Day, 1966), 6.

3. Wilfred T. Jewkes and Jerome B. Landfield, *Joan of Arc: Fact, Legend and Literature*, (New York: Harcourt, Brace & World, Inc., 1964), 53.

4. Lucien Fabre, *Joan of Arc*, translated by Gerard Hopkins (Long Acre, London: Odhams Press Limited, 1954), 57.

5. Ibid., 80.

6. Ibid., 105.

7. Fabre, 113.

8. Ibid., 116.

9. Ibid., 121.

10. Ibid., 131.

11. Ibid., 112.

12. Pernoud, 90.

13. Fabre, 160-61.

14. Jewkes and Landfield, 59.

15. Pernoud, 134.

16. Ibid., 129.

17. Ibid., 143-44.

18. Ibid., 180-81.

19. Jewkes and Landfield, 69.

20. Fabre, 286.

21. Jewkes and Landfield, 70-73.

22. Fabre, 300.

23. Pernoud, 196-97.

24. Ibid., 213-15.

25. Ibid., 213.

26. Fabre, 75.

27. Jewkes and Landfield, 79.

28. Fabre, 334-35.

29. Pernoud, 269.

30. Jewkes and Landfield, 59.

31. Hertha Pauli, *Her Name Was Sojourner Truth* (NY: Appleton-Century-Crosts, Inc., 1962), 21.

32. Mary Hovanec, "Sojourner Truth," in *African American Women: A Biographical Dictionary*, ed. Dorothy C. Salem (New York: Garland Publishing, 1993), 514. See also Hertha Pauli cited above, page 23. Ms. Pauli does not actually say Dumont fathered Isabella's child, but she frequently mentions that Isabella's daughter Diana had lighter skin than her mother.

33. James Clyde Sellman, "Sojourner Truth," in *Africana: The Encyclopedia of the African and African American Experience*, eds. Kwame Anthony Appiah, Henry Louis Gates, Jr. (New York: Civitas Books, 1999), 1888.

34. Jacqueline Bernard, *Journey Toward Freedom: The Story of Sojourner Truth* (New York: W. W. Norton and Company, Inc., 1967), 48.

35. Margaret Washington, ed., *Narrative of Sojourner Truth* (New York: Vintage Books of Random House, 1993), reprint from 1850 edition, printed in Boston and New York, 69.

36. Pauli, 123.

37. Washington, 80.

38. Ibid., 90.

39. Ibid., 94.

40. Bernard, 135.

41. Pauli, 176.

42. Ibid, 172-73.

43. Ibid., 163.

44. Bernard, 167.

45. Ibid., 183.

46. Pauli, 203.

47. Bernard, 188-89.

48. Ibid., 211.

49. Elizabeth Cady Stanton, Susan B. Anthony, and Matilda Joslyn Gage, eds., *History of Woman Suffrage*, vol. 2 (New York: Fowler and Wells, 1881-1922), 222.

50. Bernard, 242-43.

51. Pauli, 207.

52. Aimee Semple McPherson, *This is That*, 1923; reprint (Los Angeles, CA: Foursquare Publications, 1996), 44.

53. Edith L. Blumhofer, *Aimee Semple McPherson: Everybody's Sister* (Grand Rapids, MI: William B. Eerdmans Publishing Co., 1993), 80.

54. Ibid., 99-100.

55. Ibid., 116.

56. Daniel Mark Epstein, *Sister Aimee: The Life of Aimee Semple McPherson* (New York: Harcourt Brace Jovanovich, 1993), 128-29.

57. Epstein, 216.

58. McPherson, 97.

59. McPherson, 421.

60. Ibid., 323.

61. Epstein, 233.

62. Blumhofer, 418-26.

63. Ibid., 174.

64. McPherson, 405, as reported in the Daily Press, Arkansas City, Kansas, May 29, 1922.

65. Blumhofer, 270.

66. Ibid., 182.

67. William G. McLoughlin, "Aimee Semple McPherson," in *Notable American Women 1607-1950*, vol. 2, ed. Edward T. James, Janet Wilson James, Paul S. Boyer (Cambridge, MA: The Belknap Press of Harvard University Press, 1971), 479.

68. Blumhofer, 176.

69. Epstein, 300.

70. Ibid., 299.

71. Ibid., 307.

72. Blumhofer, 327-28.

73. Ibid., 339-40.

74. Epstein, 395.

75. Ibid., 406.

76. Blumhofer, 369-70.

77. Epstein, 438.

78. McPherson, 332.

79. Ibid., 378.

80. *Newsweek*, 28 December 1935, 22.

81. *Newsweek*, 28 December 1935, 22.

82. *American Magazine*, April 1926, 71-2.

83. "Terror's Troth," *Time*, 10 January 1938, 49.

84. *Time*, 30 December 1935, 19.

85. "Terror's Troth," *Time*, 10 January 1938, 49.

86. Uldine Utley, *Why I am a Preacher*, Women in American Protestant Religion 1800-1930, ed. Carolyn De Swarte Gifford and Donald W. Dayton (New York: Fleming H. Revell Company, 1931; reprint, New York: Garland Publishing, Inc., 1987), 77-78.

87. Corrie ten Boom, *Father ten Boom, God's Man* (Old Tapping, NJ: Fleming H. Revell Company, 1977), 22.

88. Sam Wellman, *Corrie ten Boom, Heroine of Harlem* (Uhrichsville, OH: Barbour Publishing, Inc., 1995), 64.

89. Carole C. Carlson, *Corrie ten Boom, Her Life, Her Faith* (Old Tappan, NJ: Fleming H. Revell Company, 1983), 68-69.

90. Corrie ten Boom, John and Elizabeth Sherrill, *The Hiding Place* in *Corrie ten Boom, Her Story* (New York: Inspirational Press, 1995), 58.

91. Carlson, 116-17.

92. Corrie ten Boom and Jamie Buckingham, *Tramp for the Lord*, in *Corrie ten Boom, Her Story* (New York: Inspiration Press, 1995), 199.

93. Ibid., 217-18.

94. Ibid., 221.

95. Carlson, 151.

96. Ten Boom, *Tramp for the Lord*, 227.

97. Ibid., 184.

98. Carlson, 171.

99. Helen Kooiman Hosier, *Kathryn Kuhlman* (Old Tappan, NJ: Fleming H. Revell Company, 1976), 36.

100. Wayne E. Warner, *Kathryn Kuhlman: The Woman Behind the Miracles* (Ann Arbor, MI: Servant Publications, 1993), 34.

101. Ibid., 34.

102. Hosier, 64.

103. Warner, 92-94.

104. Allen Spraggett, *Kathryn Kuhlman: The Woman Who Believes in Miracles* (New York: New American Library, 1970), 114.

105. Hosier, 67.

106. Kathryn Kuhlman, *I Believe in Miracles* (Englewood Cliffs, NJ: Prentice-Hall, Inc., 1962), 38-43.

107. Warner, 158.

108. Hosier, 134-35.

109. Charles Moritz, ed. *Current Biography Yearbook 1974* (New York: The H. W. Wilson Company, 1974), 228.

110. Buckingham, 179.

111. Warner, 179-84.

112. Hosier, 136-37.

113. Ibid., 133-34.

114. Warner, 163-66.

115. Ibid., 223-24.

116. Buckingham, 70-71.

117. Ibid., 221-24.

118. Kuhlman, 215.

119. Buckingham, 257.

120. Ibid., 150.

121. "Miracle Woman," Time 14 Sept. 1970, 62

122. Hosier, 126.

123. Warner, 196.

124. Buckingham, 153.

125. Ibid., 270-72.

126. *Christianity Today*, 5.

127. Hosier, 70.

Works Cited

American Magazine, April 1926, 71-2.

Bernard, Jacqueline. *Journey Toward Freedom: The Story of Sojourner Truth*. New York: W. W. Norton and Company, Inc., 1967.

Blau, Eleanor. "Evangelist Draws Sick and Anguished." *New York Times*, 20 October 1972, 45.

Blumhofer, Edith L. *Aimee Semple McPherson: Everybody's Sister*. Grand Rapids, MI: William B. Eerdmans Publishing Co., 1993.

Buckingham, Jamie. *Daughter of Destiny: Kathryn Kuhlman...Her Story*. Plainfield, NJ: Logos International, 1976.

Carlson, Carole C. *Corrie ten Boom, Her Life, Her Faith*. Old Tappan, NJ: Fleming H. Revell Company, Inc., 1983.

Epstein, Daniel Mark. *Sister Aimee: The Life of Aimee Semple McPherson*. New York: Harcourt Brace Jovanovich, 1993.

Fabre, Lucien. *Joan of Arc*. Translated by Gerard Hopkins. Long Acre, London: Odhams Press Limited, 1954.

Fauset, Arthur Huff. *Sojourner Truth: God's Faithful Pilgrim*. New York: Russell & Russell, 1938.

"Healing in the Spirit." *Christianity Today*, 20 July 1973, 4-10.

Hosier, Helen Kooiman. *Kathryn Kuhlman*. Old Tappan, NJ: Fleming H. Revell Company, 1976.

Hovanec, Mary. "Sojourner Truth." In *African American Women: A Biographical Dictionary*. Ed. Dorothy C. Salem. New York: Garland Publishing, 1993.

Jewkes, Wilfred T. and Jerome B. Landfield, *Joan of Arc: Fact, Legend, and Literature*. New York: Harcourt, Brace and World, Inc., 1964.

Kuhlman, Kathryn. *I Believe in Miracles*. Englewood Cliffs, NJ: Prentice-Hall, Inc., 1962.

McLoughlin, William G. "Aimee Semple McPherson." In *Notable American Women 1607-1950*. Vol. 2. Ed. Edward T. James, Janet Wilson James, Paul S. Boyer. Cambridge, MA: The Belknap Press of Harvard University Press, 1971.

McPherson, Aimee Semple. *This is That*. 1923; reprint, Los Angeles, CA: Foursquare Publications, 1996.

"Miracle Woman." *Time*, 14 September 1970, 62.

Moritz, Charles, ed. *Current Biography Yearbook 1974*. New York: The H. W. Wilson Company, 1974.

Morris, James. *The Preachers*. New York: St. Martin's Press, 1973.

Newsweek, 28 December 1935, 22.

Pauli, Hertha. *Her Name Was Sojourner Truth.* New York: Appleton-Century-Crosts, Inc., 1962.

Pernoud, Regine. *Joan of Arc.* Translated by Edward Hyams. New York: Stein and Day, 1966.

Sellman, James Clyde. "Sojourner Truth." In *Africana: The Encyclopedia of the African and African American Experience.* Eds. Kwame Anthony Appiah and Henry Louis Gates, Jr. New York: Civitas Books, 1999.

Spraggett, Allen. *Kathryn Kuhlman: The Woman Who Believes in Miracles.* New York: New American Library, 1970.

Stanton, Elizabeth Cady, Susan B. Anthony, and Matilda Joslyn Gage, eds. *History of Woman Suffrage.* Vol. 2. New York: Fowler and Wells, 1881-1922.

Ten Boom, Corrie, *Father ten Boom, God's Man.* Old Tapping, NJ: Fleming H. Revell Company, 1977.

Ten Boom, Corrie and Jamie Buckingham. *Tramp for the Lord.* In *Corrie ten Boom, Her Story.* New York: Inspirational Press, 1995.

Ten Boom, Corrie, John and Elizabeth Sherrill. *The Hiding Place.* In *Corrie ten Boom, Her Story.* New York: Inspirational Press, 1995.

"Terror's Troth." *Time*, 10 January 1938, 49.

Thomas, Lately. *Storming Heaven: The Lives and Turmoils of Minnie Kennedy and Aimee Semple McPherson.* New York: William Morrow and Company, 1970.

Time, 30 December 1935, 19.

Utley, Uldine. *Why I am a Preacher*. Women in American Protestant Religion 1800-1930. Ed. Carolyn De Swarte Gifford and Donald W. Dayton. New York: Fleming H. Revell Company, 1931; reprint, New York: Garland Publishing, Inc., 1987.

Warner, Wayne E. *Kathryn Kuhlman. The Woman Behind the Miracles*. Ann Arbor, MI: Servant Publications, 1993.

Washington, Margaret, ed. *Narrative of Sojourner Truth*. New York: Vintage Books of Random House, 1993. Reprint from 1850 edition, printed in Boston and New York.

Wellman, Sam. *Corrie ten Boom, Heroine of Harlem*. Uhrichsville, OH: Barbour Publishing, Inc., 1995.